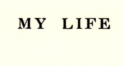

MY LIFE

A. Bebel.

MY LIFE

BY

AUGUST BEBEL

New York · HOWARD FERTIG · 1973

First published in 1912

HOWARD FERTIG, INC. EDITION 1973

Library of Congress Cataloging in Publication Data

Bebel, August, 1840–1913.
  My life.

  Translation of Aus meinem Leben.
  Reprint of the 1912 ed.
  I. Title.
HX273.B42   1972   335'.0092'4   [B]   74–80614

PRINTED IN THE UNITED STATES OF AMERICA
BY NOBLE OFFSET PRINTERS, INC.

PREFACE

To my English Readers

IT is with pleasure that I accede to the request of my English publishers, that I should address a few words to my English readers by way of introduction to the English version of my Recollections.

I imagine the purpose of memoirs is to make plain to the public the motives and circumstances which influence a man who comes to play an influential part in a certain period and sphere of action, and to contribute to a clearer comprehension of certain contemporary events.

It is my personal conviction that even the most remarkable and influential of men is more often the thing driven than the driving power ; that he can do little more than help into being that which in a given state of society is pressing onward to the realisation and recognition which are essentially its due. This being my belief, I have been saved from regarding my own activities as anything more than those of a willing helper at a birth of whose origin he is entirely innocent.

Into the rôle of an assistant at a historical process of evolution I was thrust by the conditions of my life and as a result of my experience. Once driven into the movement that originated in the 'sixties of the last century among the German working-classes, it was my duty and my interest, not only to take part in the conflict of opinions born of this movement, but also to examine the ideas which were then newly emerging, and as judiciously as I could to decide for or against them. It was thus that in the course of a few years from being a convinced and decided opponent of Socialism I became one of its most zealous adherents. I was a Saul, and became a Paul ; and a Paul I have remained even unto the evening of my life, more than ever convinced of the justice of my beliefs, and so I shall remain to the end, as long as my strength is left me.

What I must call the proletarianisation of the masses, which is steadily progressing, and resulting in a continually aggravated class antagonism, being the result of the industrial development of the last fifty years, with capitalism on the large scale as its basis, has produced that class of humanity whose interests, becoming ever more sharply opposed to the existing economic order, drive them into the ranks of Social-Democracy—the modern working-class. But for this gigantic economic development and its consequences I myself, with others who share my convictions, might have spoken with the tongues of angels, but we should have produced no effect whatever. As a result of this development, however, I—and I will not deny all personal merit in the matter— became, with the help of certain others, the leader of the German Social-Democratic party, which is at present the strongest party of that colour in the world ; a party which, directly and indirectly, influences both the internal and external policy of the German Empire, and that to a greater extent than its opponents care to own. The late Chancellor of the Empire, Count Caprivi, was the only statesman of his time honest enough to confess that the Government carefully considered every Bill it laid before the Reichstag in the light of its possible influence on Social-Democracy. And no one familiar with German conditions will doubt that, failing the existence of a strong Social-Democratic party, the foreign policy of Germany would have been far more aggressive than it has been.

It may interest the English reader of these Recollections to learn something of the manner in which the German Social-Democratic party attained its present powerful position. The present instalment of my Recollections stops at the autumn of 1878: at which time, after the two attempts on the life of the Emperor William, Prince Bismarck thought it expedient to force a strong Coercion Bill through the Reichstag: a measure which, directed against the Social-Democratic party, after remaining in force for twelve years (until 1891), proved utterly ineffectual, and cost the Chancellor his office.

Prince Bismarck had hoped by this Coercion Bill, if not to suppress, at least to retard the development of the party. Yet he was to see this party, after the suppression of its Press and organisation, increase the number of its votes from 312,000 in 1881 to 1,427,000 in 1890, by which time it had become the strongest party in Germany. This increase of power conclusively demonstrated that his coercive legislation was ineffectual and superfluous. Not Social-Democracy but Bismarck was vanquished, and his defeat was sealed by his dismissal.

It was thus manifest that the same forces which had crowned our propaganda with success after success before the passing of the anti-Socialist laws continued to operate even more powerfully after those laws were put into force. And they are still operating at the present day, as is proved by the last elections to the Reichstag, those of January, 1912, when the party obtained no less than 4,250,000 votes and sent 110 members to the Reichstag, a success unique in the light of the fact that 99 per cent. of the members of the party are working-men. The characteristic point in this development is the fact that from 1881 onwards— that being the date of the first election fought under the anti-Socialist laws—although the number of seats won by the party fluctuated, the number of votes steadily increased : a point to which the party attaches decisive importance as a measure of real growth and a sure sign that it is striking root more deeply than ever amidst the lower classes.

This success was possible only at the price of an intensive and uninterrupted propaganda with the object of enlightening the masses ; a labour which demanded enormous sacrifices of time, energy, and money, and the creation of a magnificent organisation, which, in its turn, could only have resulted from the co-operation of a multiplicity of forces. That I have to the best of my power contributed to this success I will not deny.

A. BEBEL.

Schöneberg-Berlin,
June, 1912.

CONTENTS

CONTENTS 13

MY LIFE

CHAPTER I

CHILDHOOD AND YOUTH

EVERY ONE is born somewhere. I enjoyed this advantage on the 22nd February of 1840, when I saw the light in the casemates of Deutz-Koeln. My father, Johann Gottlob Bebel, was a non-commissioned officer of the 3rd company of the 25th Regiment of Infantry. My mother was Wilhelmina Johanna, *née* Simon.

It is not superfluous, because essential to the comprehension of my character, to say something of my father and mother. My father, who was born in Ostrowo, in the Province of Posen, was the son of a cooper. I think I am right in assuming that the Bebels migrated eastwards from the south-west of Germany about the time of the Reformation. I know for certain that a Bebel lived in Kreuzburg, Silesia, as early as 1625 ; but they are still more numerous in south-west Germany. The explanation of my father's return to the west of Germany was that he, together with his twin-

brother August, my godfather, had enlisted in one
of the Prussian-Polish regiments ; but the Prussian
Government, when the Polish insurrection broke
out in 1830, thought it best to remove these regiments from the Province of Posen.   Thus my
father's regiment became attached to the then
Federal fortress of Mayence.   This move enabled
my father to make my mother's acquaintance.

My mother came of a not unprosperous family
of the lower middle class, which had been settled
for a long time in the formerly free imperial city
of Wetzlar.   Her father was a baker and peasant-
farmer.   As the family was large my mother went
into service in Frankfort.   From Frankfort she
went to Mayence, and there came to know my
father.   When later on my father's regiment was
again stationed at Posen my father, to please his
future wife, and perhaps also because he liked the
Rhineland better than the country of his birth,
procured an exchange into the 25th Regiment of
the line, in garrison at Koeln-Deutz.   His twin-
brother August, my godfather, followed his example,
exchanging into the 40th Regiment of the line, then
stationed at Mayence.

The family of a Prussian non-commissioned
officer of that time had to live under miserable
conditions.   The pay was more than scanty.   All
the military and official classes of Prussia had in

those days to exist on very narrow means ; almost every one had to go hungry, tightening his belt for God, king, and country. There is truth in the saying that Prussia became great by hunger. My mother had some sort of canteen licence—that is, she had a permit to sell a variety of miscellaneous goods and provisions to the soldiers. The counter was in our one and only room. I still see her by the light of her rape-oil lamp filling the earthenware bowls of the soldiers with steaming hot potatoes at the price of one halfpenny a portion. For us children—I had in the meantime acquired a brother—life in the casemates was full of enjoyment. We ran in and out of the rooms, petted and teased by sergeants and soldiers. I used to go, when the men were out, to the room of Sergeant Wintermann, who was my godfather, where I would take his guitar from its peg ; indeed, I practised until all the strings were broken. To give these unbridled exercises a less destructive direction my godfather cut from a plank of wood a guitar-shaped instrument fitted with strings. Then I would sit for hours, together with my brother, at the entrance to a courtyard in the Haupstrasse of Deutz, maltreating the strings in a way which so delighted the daughters of a squadron commander, who lived in a house across the road, that they used to regale us at times with cake and sweetmeats as a reward

for my performance.   Naturally, military drill was
not allowed to suffer to the profit of these musical
exercises ;   the whole environment incited to it ;
it was literally in the air.

But my father gradually came to look at soldier-
ing with very different eyes.   He was, indeed, as
my mother often told us, a quite exceptionally
smart, punctual, and conscientious soldier ;   but he
had by then seen twelve years or more of military
service, and had had enough of it and to spare.
Evidently he did not lack the independence and
the spirit of opposition which in those days found
such a favourable soil in the Province of the
Rhine.   More than once he returned home to our
dull casemate chamber in raging anger and with
curses on his lips.   When after fifteen years of
service he was prostrated for many months in the
military hospital suffering from a serious illness,
with death and the subsequent destitution of his
family staring him in the face, he warned our
mother repeatedly and most earnestly not to send
his boys, after his death, to the military orphanage,
because entrance therein imposed the obligation
of nine years' active service in the army.   Fearing
that our mother might yet act thus from sheer
necessity, in his excitement, intensified by his
illness, he repeatedly cried out, " If you do it, I
will stab the boys in front of the company," quite
forgetting that he would then be dead.

In a sense my father found salvation when, in the opening of 1843, he was offered the post of frontier-guard. He accepted, and, with his family, travelled sometimes afoot, sometimes on the wagon which carried the household furniture, for in those days there was no railway, to Hertzogenrad, a town on the Belgian frontier.

But there was no abiding for us. Before the and of the three months' probation my father became seriously ill, as a result of the hard night watches. My mother called his malady inflammation of the muscles ; I suppose it was rheumatism ; at all events, consumption supervened. As my father had not finished his period of probation, he had not yet attained his discharge from military service, and we had to return to Cologne, making the journey back as we had come, with my father suffering severely. These were hard times for my mother.

In Cologne my father was sent to the military hospital, while my mother was given a casemate-room. After thirteen months my father died, at the age of thirty-five, leaving my mother without a claim to a pension. Soon after his death we had to leave the casemate, and my mother would have been forced to return to her birthplace, Wetzlar, but for my father's twin-brother, August Bebel, who took care of her and us boys. The better to fulfil

this duty, he determined, in the autumn of 1844,
to marry my mother. My stepfather had obtained
his discharge in September, 1841, on account of
a loss of voice resulting from inflammation of the
larynx, which later developed into consumption.
He received a "compassionate grant" of two
thalers (about six shillings) per month. After that
he was for two years a constable to the military
hospital at Mayence, and afterwards a warder in
the reformatory of Brauweiler, near Cologne. We
settled in Brauweiler in the late summer of 1844.
The reformatory formed a large aggregation of
buildings and yards and gardens, surrounded by,
a high wall. Men, women, and juvenile offenders
were separated. To get to the prison building,
where we had our lodgings, we had to cross several
of the yards, opening several heavy bolted doors.
The prison was completely shut off from all outside
humanity. At night, as soon as dusk set in, dozens
of owls of all sizes would fly round the buildings,
screeching and hooting, to the terror of my brother
and myself. These owls nested in the churchyard
near by. Apart from that, this home was far from
pleasing to us children ; it was, I should imagine,
no more acceptable to our parents. For the
prisoners were cruelly treated ; their groans and
screams rang through the whole building, naturally
terrifying my brother and myself.

Here in Brauweiler I was sent, when only some five years of age, to the village school.

Life was very monotonous, confined, as it was for the most part, within the prison walls. Our father, by nature severe, was easily irritated, a tendency aggravated by his increasing illness—consumption. Mother and children both suffered much from this cause. More than once my mother had to stay his hands when he, beside himself with exasperation, had commenced to thrash us. If corporal punishment were the highest emanation of educational wisdom, I should have become a paragon. But who would dare to assert as much? Whatever I am, I am in spite of caning.

On the other hand, our father really did his best for us, for he was at bottom a good-hearted man. For example, to make us happy at Christmas, New Year, or Easter, he would go as far as our modest means would allow ; and these were very modest indeed. In addition to free lodgings (two rooms), fuel, and light, my father received eight thalers (twenty-four shillings) monthly pay. This had to provide for five persons.

My father's malady made rapid progress, and he died on the 19th of October, 1846. My brother and I felt the death of our stepfather as a deliverance from oppression. The terrible severity with which he punished every expression of self which he thought improper made us tremble as soon as he came in sight. He made us fear him. Love for him we never felt. How my mother took the loss of her second husband I do not know; but hers was not a happy marriage. From this second marriage again she derived no claim to a pension. Nothing remained but to return to her birthplace, Wetzlar. In the beginning of November we once more loaded our possessions on a wagon, and set out for Cologne. The weather was severe, cold, and rainy. In Cologne our furniture was put on the roadway, close to the river front, to be transported by ship as far as Coblenz, and hence again by wagon up the valley of the River Lahn to Wetzlar. We arrived there the fifth or sixth day.

In Wetzlar there lived our grandmother and three sisters and a brother of my mother's—all married. It was there that we spent our later childhood. I was first sent to the Poor Law School, which occupied a house that had once belonged to the Knights of the Teutonic Order. In the courtyard there still stands the one-storied house where dwelt Charlotte Buff, the heroine of Goethe's "Werther." Later on, as it happened, I several times slept in this house, as one of my cousins was the cicerone attached to the Charlotte Buff room. I well remember the celebration of the anniversary of Goethe's hundredth birthday in

1849, near the Wildbach fountain, which was thenceforth called the Goethe Fountain. Ten years later I was present at the celebration of Schiller's hundredth birthday in the Municipal Theatre of Salzburg.

Some years later the Poor Law School was incorporated with the Citizen School (Public Elementary School). We—the former Poor Law boys—were then called *Freischüler* (free scholars).

At school I got on well enough with my teachers. I was among the best scholars, so that my geometry teacher, an excellent little man, undertook to initiate me and two other boys into the secrets of mathematics. We even learned to use logarithms. Next to arithmetic and geometry, my favourite studies were history and geography. Religious instruction, which had no meaning for me, I did not much care for, and my mother—an enlightened and liberal-minded woman—did not bother us with it at home. I learned only because I had to. Though amongst the best pupils, I sometimes gave our *Ober-Pfarrer* (head pastor) answers which did not fit into his philosophy and earned me friendly reprimands. While I was a good scholar, and in all subjects amongst the foremost, I was also the first at playing all sorts of pranks, and thus I earned the reputation of being a moral reprobate :

especially with our *Kantor* (singing master), whose
task it was—I know not why, if not on account of
his large girth, or his seniority, or by reason of
some customary right—to avenge upon the
miscreants all the pranks that were denounced
in school to the headmaster.

My bad reputation with the Kantor became
gradually so firmly rooted that he took my participation in every kind of devilry for granted.
If to save a comrade from unjust punishment I
undertook to plead for him, I at once became
suspect and shared in the punishment, even though
absolutely innocent.   Later on, in party matters,
this characteristic trait of mine—to be just at any
cost—got me the nickname of *Gerechtigkeitsmeier*
(Just-at-any-price-man).   More often than not our
Kantor was quite justified in passing judgment
on me.

Yet for me, too, the day of knowledge came,
when I told myself, " Now you must begin to be
a sensible fellow."   It happened thus : The son of
the major of the Rifle Battalion stationed at Wetzlar
was my comrade in many an escapade.   The day
of the examination came round, the public consisting solely of my friend's father, who was a
veritable giant.   The examination came to an end,
and the marks obtained were read out.   These
depended, curiously enough, on good conduct alone.

All the scholars heard their marks announced, except my friend and myself. We alone obtained five marks apiece—that is, the minimum. The Major did not wince, but I knew that my chum would get no soft words at home. Since that day I have never seen him again. He was immediately sent to the Military School. Later on I heard that he had attained high military rank, so that being a bad boy at school had done him as little harm as it did me. But from that hour I was a good boy—that is, I did nothing that would be punishable. At the next examination I took the third place, and at the next and last the first place. By the verdict of my form I should even have secured one of the prizes that were given away. When the headmaster was on the point of announcing the name of the second prize-winner the whole class shouted my name. The rector said I had reformed, but not enough to deserve a prize ; so I stepped out into life unrewarded.

Our circumstances could not improve in Wetzlar. My mother had no claim to a pension : the only grant she received from the Government at a later date was some eighteenpence per month for each of us two boys. This was granted her because, in spite of the warning of her first husband, she had sent in our names to the Military Orphanage at Potsdam. It was poverty that forced her to do so. To enable us to live she had already sold several of the small plots of land which she had inherited from her mother. It was very hard for her to bring herself to this, for she had set her heart upon leaving us intact what still remained, so that we should not be quite penniless after her death. What sacrifices a mother will make for her children I learned from my own mother. For a time she sewed white military gloves for her brother-in-law, a glovemaker, at the rate of about twopence the pair. She could not finish more than one pair a day—not enough to live on, yet too much to die on; but even this work she had to give up after two years, for she, too, in the meantime had contracted consumption, which in her last years made any and every work impossible. I, the eldest boy, had to do the housework, make the coffee, clean the rooms, and scrub them every Saturday. I had to clean the pewter plates and the kitchen utensils, and make the beds, and so on, an experience which stood me in good stead in later days when on the road in search of work and as a political prisoner. When my mother had even to give up cooking we used to take our dinner with an aunt; for our mother we fetched what little food she needed from several families better off than our own. I then resolved to earn some money, and obtained employment as boy in a skittle-alley. After school I used to go to a skittle-alley in a garden restaurant, where I set up the skittles after every throw. I did not reach home till nearly ten o'clock, and on Sundays not until much later. The stooping made my back ache so much that I used to go home groaning, and in the end I had to give it up. Another occupation for us boys in the autumn was loading potatoes into sacks in the fields belonging to one of our aunts. It was not very pleasant work—from seven in the morning until dusk, in cold, wet, and foggy weather; we obtained in payment a big bag of potatoes to tide over the winter, and every morning before going to the fields we were given as a stimulant a big slice of plum-cake, of which we were passionately fond.

When I was thirteen, and my brother twelve, my brother was notified that he could enter the Military Orphanage. I had not passed the military inspection, and was declared unfit for service. But now my mother lost courage. Feeling her end near, she would not take the responsibility of allowing my brother to enlist for nine years, after two years' free military education. " If you wish to be soldiers, do it later on voluntarily ; I will not be responsible now," she said. So my brother did not go to the Orphanage. As for myself, I was sorry to have been rejected.

My childish imagination was stirred by the revolutionary years of '48 and '49. The majority of the citizens of Wetzlar, in accordance with the traditions of the town, had republican sympathies. These sympathies were shared by the school-children. Once, I remember, when a number of boys were disputing after their fashion on matters political, it happened that only two boys, of whom I was one, declared themselves Monarchists, a luxury which earned us a sound thrashing. When next my political opponents wax indignant over my anti-patriotic views, because in their opinion the Monarchy and the Fatherland are identical, let them remember that I suffered for the Father-land when their fathers and grandfathers were still, in the innocence of their youth, anti-patriots. In the Rhine Province of that period the majority of the population was republican.

We boys were greatly interested in the peasant revolts which broke out in those years in the neigh-bourhood of Wetzlar. The peasants were then still subject to all sorts of servitude, the relics of the feudal ages. Now, when all men were full of thoughts of liberty and equality, the peasants, too, wanted to free themselves from this oppression. They gathered in their thousands and marched to the castle of the Prince of Solms-Braunfels. They marched, as a rule, under a large black and white flag—the Prussian colours—as a sign that they were willing to be Prussians, but never Braunfelsians. Some of the mob were armed with guns, but the great majority had only scythes, pitchforks, axes, and so on. Behind the processions, which were several times repeated but never resulted in bloodshed, marched the garrison of Wetzlar, to protect the Prince. As to the town militia, which during these years made its appearance in Wetzlar also, I regarded it with undisguised contempt, on account of its utter lack of military smartness.

The year 1853 made us orphans. My mother died in June. She looked death in the face with calm heroism. When on the afternoon of the day of her death she felt that her end was near she asked us to call her sisters, without giving us any reason for her wish. When her sisters came we were sent out of the room. Sorrowfully we sat for hours on the staircase and waited for something to happen. At last, towards seven o'clock, her sisters came out of the room and told us that our mother was dead. The same evening we had to pack our things and follow our aunts, without having seen our dead mother. Poor woman ! she had few happy days, either as wife or widow ; and yet she was always bright and of good cheer. In the space of three years she had buried two husbands and had lost two children. She had many

anxieties on account of illness. In 1848 I fell ill
with typhoid fever, and for many weeks hovered
between life and death. Some years later I was
threatened with lameness, but escaped with straight
limbs. My brother, when he was nine years of
age, fell from the top of a ladder, and suffered
from concussion of the brain as well as a severe
scalp wound. He escaped death by the skin of
his teeth. My mother suffered from consumption
for at least seven years. Few mothers can have
suffered more sorrow and tribulation.

I now went to an aunt of mine, who held in
fee-simple a water-mill ; my brother to another
aunt, whose husband was a baker. I had to make
myself useful in the mill. I liked best to drive
our two donkeys to the peasants in the country,
taking them flour and bringing back grain. In
addition to the donkeys my aunt had a horse,
two cows, a number of pigs, and some dozen
fowls. She did a little farming, so there was
no lack of work, though there was a son to help
her, and two servants were kept, a man and a
woman. When the men had no time for the
purpose I had to groom the horse and the donkeys,
and sometimes to ride the horse to water. The
poultry-yard was left to my sole care ; I had to
feed the fowls, collect the eggs, and clean out the
fowlhouse. Amid these occupations the Easter of

1854 approached. I was at the end of my school-days, a fact which I regarded with very mixed feelings. I should very greatly have preferred to remain at school.

CHAPTER II

APPRENTICE AND JOURNEYMAN

" Now, what do you want to do? " my guardian asked me—he was one of my uncles.

" I should like to be a mining engineer."

" What ! have you the money for your studies? "
This question dispelled my dream.

I had answered " a mining engineer " because ironstone mining had lately been developed in the neighbourhood of Wetzlar. As this was out of the question I decided to become a turner, for no better reason than the fact that the husband of a friend of my mother's was a master-turner of good repute, and willing to take me as an apprentice. Although I was by no means a block-head, I never, to tell the truth, became an artist at the lathe. As a matter of fact, I was hampered by physical inefficiency ; as a boy I was always very weak and insufficiently nourished. For many years our supper used to consist of a fair-sized piece of bread smeared with a little butter or jam.

When we complained of hunger—and that we did every day—our mother would always reply, "One has sometimes to close the sack even if it is not quite full." It will thus be understood that for years my highest ambition was just once to eat my fill of bread and butter.

My master and his wife were very decent and respectable people. The food was good, though not very plentiful. The work was hard and the hours long; I started at 5 a.m. and worked until 7 p.m., with hardly any break; from the bench we went to a hasty meal and back again to the bench. The first thing in the morning I had to fetch water from a distant well, and for this I received from the mistress some three-halfpence a week—the only pocket-money I ever had during my apprenticeship. I was out of doors rarely during the week, hardly ever in the evening, and never without special permission. It was the same on Sundays, because Sunday was our principal day of business, for then the farmers came to town to make their purchases and to get their repairs done; only towards evening was I at liberty for two or three hours. On Sunday mornings I was allowed to go to church; but as I did not care for the privilege I used to play truant, taking good care to discover the number of the hymn to be sung and the name of the preacher for the day, so that I should not be entrapped by questions. However, in the end I was caught, and my master said dryly that as I did not seem to care for church I had better stay at home. Losing thus another slice of liberty, I turned all the more eagerly to the reading of books, which, as there was no one to guide my reading, were naturally for the most part romances. I had read "Robinson Crusoe" and "Uncle Tom's Cabin" while still at school. Now my favourite author was Hackländer, a writer of stories of military life in peace time. My enthusiasm for things military was greatly cooled by his books. I also read the novels of Sir Walter Scott, and of certain German historical novelists. From my home days I had saved a few historical works, such as a short history of Greece and Rome, and some volumes of Prussian history, from which I learned by heart the dates of all the Prussian kings, famous generals, battles, and so forth.

I impatiently looked forward to the end of my apprentice days, for I longed to see the world. But I did not see it as soon as I had hoped. On the last day of my bondage my master died, and as his wife had no one else to look to, and had decided to liquidate the business, I determined to stay with her and help her, for she had always been very good to me. I worked hard from May until

August, from sunrise until nine o'clock at night. At last, towards the end of January, 1858, the business was sold, and I was able to set out on my travels. My mistress gave me a present of 3s. as well as my wages of 1s. 6d. per week. On the 1st of February I set out on foot, my brother giving me his company for a few miles of the way. When we parted he wept bitterly, which was quite unlike him. I never saw him again; he died in the summer of 1859, after a short illness. I was left alone, the last of the family.

I went first to Frankfort, where I spent two days, thence by railway to Heidelberg. Artisans on the tramp had in those days to carry passports, which had to be stamped by the police at the various stations on the road, and evasions of this rule were punished. In many cities—in Heidelberg, for example—they had to attend at the police-station in order to submit to a medical examination, more especially for contagious affections of the skin. From Heidelberg I went to Mannheim, and thence to Spires, where I found work. I was well treated, and the food was good, but I had to sleep in a corner of the workshop. It was then the general custom for the journeymen to lodge and board with the master. The wages were low—some 2s. per week—but when I complained the master told me that he himself had started life on the same wages. That, however, was fifteen years earlier.

It was at Spires that, being foolish enough to sit down to a game of cards, I lost at one sitting a sum of 18 kreuzers, or some six pence—nearly a quarter of my weekly wage! I swore never again to play for money, and have kept this pledge all my life.

Spring saw me on the road again. I tramped all through the Palatinate, passing through Landau and Karlsruhe, and many another city, until at last I came to Freiburg, in the south of Baden; there I spent a very agreeable summer. Freiburg, as regards its position, is one of the most favoured of German towns, surrounded as it is with magnificent forests and many beauty spots which invite excursions. But I greatly missed the society of young people in circumstances similar to my own. The trade guilds had been dissolved, and as yet the trades unions had not come into existence; neither were there any political clubs which a workman might join. For clubs of a purely social nature I had neither money nor inclination. It was at this time that I first became aware of the existence of the so-called Catholic Artisans Union (*Katholische Gesellenverein*), which had its own clubhouse in Freiburg. After making sure that the club was open to non-Catholics, I became a member.

As long as I lived in South Germany and Austria I was a member of these Catholic Unions, and I never had cause to regret it. There was no intolerance in respect of members of a different religious persuasion. The presidents were everywhere priests, and the members elected a senior member as their own representative. Lectures were given and classes held in various subjects— French, for instance—so that these Unions were to a certain extent educational institutions. In the reading-room a number of papers and journals were available; although these were exclusively Catholic, I was glad to read them, for I was greatly interested in politics. The need of the society of decent young people was equally satisfied. These clubs derived a characteristic tone from the presence of the chaplains, who, being young and full of animal spirits, were on their side glad to mix with men of their own age. I have spent many a merry evening in the company of these young curates. To this day I have preserved my book of membership, having on its first page a picture of St. Joseph, the patron saint of the Union.

In September, 1858, I left Freiburg, and walking through the Black Forest, I came to Schaffhausen, in Switzerland. Prussian subjects were at that time forbidden by their Government to enter Switzerland—firstly, on accont of political dif-

ferences, and, secondly, lest they should absorb
republican ideas. I therefore left Schaffhausen
immediately, taking boat across the Bodensce
—where I was seasick !—and after journeying
through many cities came finally to Munich. In
Munich I remained a full week, but finding no
work there, decided to leave for Ratisbon. The
first part of the journey I travelled down the
River Isar, on a raft, working my passage.

Nothing of much interest befell me at Ratisbon,
but I quarrelled with my master and left the city
on the 1st of February, notwithstanding the intense
cold. With a companion, I first returned to
Munich, intending to proceed into Austria. The
passing of the Austrian frontier was in those days
a matter of some difficulty—you had to prove to the
frontier guards the possession of at least five gulden
(about 8s.) ; as we had not so much money we
hit on the expedient of using the railway, travelling
from the last station on the Bavarian side of the
frontier into Austrian territory. To look, as far
as possible, our part as " gentlemen," we gave an
extra polish to our boots, and brushed our clothes
with especial care, while each assumed a white
collar. We were entirely successful, passing the
frontier guards unsuspected. In severe cold and
deep snow we tramped through the Tyrol, finally
arriving at Salzburg during a spell of beautiful

sunshine, enchanted by the view of the town, with its many churches and houses in the Italian style.

In later years, looking back on these periods of tramping, during which I repeatedly got wet through to the skin and chilled to the bone, I have always wondered that I was never seriously ill. I never possessed any woollen underclothing, an overcoat remained an unknown luxury, while an umbrella, in the hands of a journeyman on the road, would have been an object of derision and contempt. Often of a morning I would don my clothes, still wet from the day before and fated to get still wetter during the day. Youth triumphs over many things.

In Salzburg I found work, and there I remained up to the end of February, 1860. The summer of 1859 was beautiful ; but it was a time of war—war between Austria on the one hand and Italy and France on the other. Masses of troops passed through Salzburg, singing and jubilant, to return a few months later defeated and depressed. I was so excited by these political events that I spent all my Sundays—on weekdays I had no leisure—in the cafés, reading the papers. Prussians were then not greatly beloved in Austria, as Prussia's hesitation to come to the aid of Austria was regarded as a betrayal. But later on, when the Tyrolean Volunteer Rifles opened a recruiting office in Salzburg, the lust for adventure seized me, and I offered my services, only to be told that foreigners were not wanted. However, when I heard from home that Prussia was mobilising her troops, I resolved to enlist as a volunteer in the Fatherland. I wrote at once to my guardian asking for money to defray the expenses of the journey; but when the money arrived—six thalers, or about 18s.—peace was declared, and the war was at an end. The money, nevertheless, came in handy when in February, 1860, I resolved to return home.

I will close my reminiscences of Salzburg with a confession. Fruit-stealing was always a weakness of mine; I suppose I was the victim of some hereditary predisposition. It was not otherwise in Salzburg. The splendid peaches in the garden of the Prince-Bishop tempted me, and I fell. I do not suppose the Bishop suffered; and certainly the peaches did me no harm. And my scruples vanished when I read that St. Ambrose, who lived towards the end of the fourth century, and was Bishop of Milan, had somewhere stated: " Nature gives all goods to all men in common; for God has created all things so that all men may enjoy them in common. Thus it was Nature that gave the right to common enjoyment, while it was unjust usurpation that originated the rights of property."

Could my action be more splendidly excused, even justified?

It was in March, 1860, when, after an absence of more than two years, I found myself back in Wetzlar. When I presented myself for military service I was put back for a year on account of general debility. The same thing happened the following year, and finally I was rejected as unfit.

In Wetzlar I got work with a Jewish master of my craft; but when the fine weather came and three of my old schoolfellows urged me to take the road to Leipzig with them, I could not resist the temptation. So far I had never felt the least inclination to go to Leipzig or to Saxony, and if left to my own devices might never have gone there at all; yet in more than one respect this journey had a decisive influence on my whole future. The arbiter of a man's destiny is often no other than chance.

At this point I should like to indulge in a digression. Most emphatically I do not agree with the proposition that a man is master of his own fate. He is impelled to action by circumstances and his environment. So-called freedom of will is mere moonshine. In most cases a man cannot conceive of the consequences of his actions; only afterwards does he recognise the results to which they lead. A step to the right instead of to the left, or vice versa, might have brought him into the grasp of quite a different set of conditions, which might have been better or worse than those which he actually experiences. Whether he has taken the right or the wrong turning he can only tell afterwards, by the ensuing consequences. Very often, having no standard of judgment, he is not even aware of the alternative. The self-made man exists only in a very limited degree. Hundreds of others, men of far better qualities than the man who comes to the top, live and perish in obscurity because unfavourable circumstances have kept them down—that is, have prevented the best application and exploitation of their personal excellences. It is favouring circumstance that lifts a man to a privileged position in life. For the very many who do not reach such a position there is no seat at the table of life; and, even if circumstances be favourable, a man must show the requisite adaptability to make use of them. But there is no personal merit in that.

We travelled afoot to Weimar, and thence to Leipzig by train, arriving in that city on the 7th of May, 1860, at eleven o'clock at night. I was lucky enough to find work at once, and just of the kind by which I afterwards built up a business of my own. If I had arrived in Leipzig twenty-four hours later some one else would have got

my billet. Thus once more a lucky chance decided
my future. For the second time I worked in a
shop on a rather larger scale than usual. We were
five journeymen and an apprentice. I liked the
master and my comrades, and also the work, which
was an excellent training for me. What I did
not like was the morning coffee, which was bad,
and the dinner, which was deficient in quantity as
well as quality. Breakfast, afternoon coffee, and
supper we had to provide ourselves. We lodged
with the master, all seven together in a roomy
garret. I soon began to rebel against the food.
In a few weeks' time I got so far as to induce my
comrades to lay a common complaint before the
master, threatening to lay down our tools if he did
not give way ; in short, although none of us had
ever heard the word, we threatened a strike. After
protracted negotiations the master granted us the
right to buy our own food, making us a money
allowance as an equivalent. Later, by remaining
obstinately abed in the morning, we also obtained
the right to start work at 7 a.m. instead of 6 a.m.
Still later we induced our master to put us on
piece-work, although at first he would not hear of
it, as he feared that " scamping " would be the
result ; but in that he soon learned he was mistaken. Finally we obtained the privilege of
" living out."

CHAPTER III

I ENTER THE WORKMEN'S MOVEMENT AND PUBLIC LIFE

Towards 1860 the Conservative reaction, which had oppressed the people since 1849, began to decline, more especially by reason of the pressure of the middle-class Liberals, who, having developed their economic forces and having acquired wealth, began to take an interest in political affairs. At the same time the "German question" acquired a new vitality, and was supported with the greatest enthusiasm. The *Nationalverein* demanded the convocation of a German Parliament. The more far-sighted of the Liberals quickly recognised the importance of securing the support of the workers, and to this end lent themselves to the promotion of workers' unions, and sought to put trustworthy men at the head of them.

The German workman of those days knew next to nothing of politics. During the years of the reaction political activity was dead. There were a few workmen's clubs, but they did not meddle with politics. In some of the German States such clubs were prohibited, as they were supposed to propagate Socialism and Communism. As a matter of fact, these words meant nothing to us of the younger generation. Some of us, perhaps, may have read Weitling's writings on Communism, but these were the exception. I don't remember any one at that time in Leipzig who was acquainted with the Communist Manifesto or with Marx's and Engel's part in the revolutionary movement. It will be gathered from this that the workers of that time were not conscious of their class interests, nor of the existence of a "social question." They eagerly joined the societies which the Liberals helped them to form, and regarded the Liberal leaders as their most devoted friends.

Leipzig was then looked upon as the principal centre of Liberalism and Democracy. On the 19th of February, 1861, I attended my first public meeting. It was convoked by the President of the Polytechnical Society, a University professor, who proposed to found a "Workers' Improvement Society" (lit. Culture-Union) as a branch of the Polytechnical Society, workmen's clubs properly so called being then forbidden in Saxony. The proposal was opposed by another professor and by some of the workmen present, who demanded full independence, considering that the principal aim of the new society should be political, and that education ought to be relegated to the schools, and should form no part of the programme of a society of adults. While I did not agree with this theory, I greatly admired these workmen for daring to oppose the learned professors, and heartily wished that I had the power of speaking as they had done.

The Society was founded, and I joined the same evening. The lectures and lessons were mostly given by professors and university men. There were courses in English, French, shorthand, book-keeping, German, and arithmetic, as well as classes in singing and gymnastics. In the second year I was elected a member of the executive of twenty-four, and president of the library and the amusement section. My ambition to speak in public was soon gratified, as I found an opportunity in the debates of the executive. A friend of mine told me later that when I spoke for the first time for a few minutes in succession those seated at the table looked at one another and asked, " Who is this, that he should dare to speak like this? "

The fight for independence and the introduction of politics continued within the Society. The tactics of this opposition were not particularly skilful. For the great majority of the younger members the educational programme was of paramount interest, and they did not wish for its abolition. Finally the opposition seceded and founded a new Society—"Vorwärts." I did not join it, though many tried to persuade me to do so.

The new Society, "Vorwärts," did not restrict itself to club meetings, but also convened workers' and general meetings for the discussion of labour topics and questions of the day. The speakers at these meetings were still rather uncertain of their aims. Among the subjects of discussion were invalidity insurance for workers, the question of a universal exhibition in Germany, universal suffrage, a German Parliament for the discussion of the labour question, and, above all, the convocation of a German Labour Congress. As the same idea had been broached in Berlin and Nuremberg a committee was formed, of which I was elected a member. The *Nationalverein* was also convoking meetings at which the German question, the creation of a German fleet, the Schleswig-Holstein question, and the Prussian parliamentary conflict were subjects of discussion.

Whatever the internal condition of Prussia, the Liberals regarded that country as the only State which could bring about the unification of Germany and protect them against the domination of the masses. Bismarck knew his Liberals when he said of them, " More than they hate me they dread a revolution." He, indeed, took his instruments where he found them. He took many former Democrats of 1848 into his service ; he tried to enlist Liebknecht, who was then in London ; he did enlist Lothar Bucher, who in turn tried to secure Karl Marx as a contributor to the Prussian Government Gazette. These methods were those of Louis Napoleon, who in a masterly way exploited class antagonisms so as to prop up his system, even at the price of universal suffrage. It soon became obvious that Bismarck intended to exploit the Labour movement as against the Liberal bourgeoisie. A committee meeting was held in Leipzig to discuss matters in relation to the General Labour Congress with a delegate from Berlin—one Eichler. This man Eichler at once went the whole hog ; the workers, he said, had nothing to expect from the Liberals and the *Nationalverein;* but he was certain—and in so saying he unmasked himself as an agent of Bismarck's—that Bismarck was in favour of a universal, direct, and equal suffrage, and was even ready to advance some £9,000 or £10,000 to the Engineers' Union of Berlin to found a productive co-operative society. Now, these very same engineers were then regarded as the chief support of the Progressive Liberals. The same idea was at a later date put forward by Lassalle, whose name was then unknown to us, although he had already published what became known as the Workers' Programme. The idea of universal, direct, and equal suffrage had already been popularised by one of Bismarck's colleagues, Privy Councillor Wagener. The suggestion was to introduce it by an Order in Council. The Liberals did not at all relish the plan, thinking that it savoured too much of the methods of Napoleon III.

At a later period—in September, 1878—when Bismarck's anti-Socialist measures were being debated in Parliament, I alluded to these manœuvres, and accused Bismarck, who was then doing his best to destroy the Social-Democratic party, of having formerly attempted to exploit it for his own political ends. Bismarck admitted that Eichler had been in the pay of the police. As to Lassalle, he stated that not he, but Lassalle, had expressed a desire to open negotiations with him, though he had put no obstacles in the way of his doing so, which fact he did not regret. As a matter of fact there had been no negotiations, for what could a poor devil like Lassalle have offered him? He had felt greatly attracted by Lassalle, for he was one of the most spiritual and lovable men he had ever known. Moreover, he was no republican; his ideal was the restoration of the German Empire, an ideal in which he shared.

This rather jejune attempt to claim Lassalle as a monarchist needs no refutation: Lassalle's writings and letters sufficiently disprove it. Still, Lassalle's attitude to Bismarck was rather peculiar. Supported by his confidence in himself and his consciousness of his independent position, he thought to negotiate with Bismarck as one power with another, though in reality he had no power at his back. Which would have got the better of the other in the end we need not inquire, as the death of Lassalle in August, 1864, removed one of the parties.

Bismarck also denied that he had intended to introduce universal suffrage. I could not prove the contrary, yet Lassalle said, in his defence before the courts: "I declare to you on this solemn occasion that before another year is out Herr von Bismarck will have played the part of a Robert Peel in that he will have introduced universal suffrage."

It is hardly credible that Lassalle should have spoken thus if the matter had not been discussed during his conversations with Bismarck. It was seriously debated at the time in Conservative circles, and Bismarck was not the man to be deterred by constitutional scruples from introducing universal suffrage by an Order in Council if he thought it expedient. The masses, who had practically no political rights whatever, would assuredly not have resented it.

But I have anticipated the course of events, and must return to my narrative. We sent delegates to Berlin, and the date of the German Labour Congress, to be held at Leipzig, together with its programme, was quickly settled in consultation with the Berlin labour leaders ; but our delegates returned much disappointed with their negotiations with the Liberal leaders. When the *Nationalverein* held its various meetings in Leipzig it became evident that the workers were not wanted as members. A second delegation to Berlin left no doubt in our minds that the leaders of the Liberal party were completely out of sympathy with the Labour movement. It was then that young Ludwig Löwe, the founder of the famous arms factory of Löwe & Co., arranged a meeting with Lassalle. There our party found what they were looking for—understanding of their demands and ready sympathy. It was arranged with Lassalle to postpone the Congress until he had published his ideas as to the position of the workers in State and society in the shape of a pamphlet which was to be distributed by the Leipzig Central Committee.

I myself had left the Central Committee in November, 1862. My position in the Workers' Improvement Society absorbed all my time, interest, and energies. As I passed all my evenings in the rooms of the society I soon got to know the needs and desires of its members far better than the presidents could. I was most assiduous in proposing motions, which were almost always carried, at the sittings of the executive and the monthly meetings. This considerably increased my influence. At that time I was still a worker; I worked at the lathe from 6 a.m. to 7 p.m., with an interval of only two hours for meals. Moreover, the debates of the Central Committee and the speeches at the meetings seemed to me rather hazy and aimless, so that I left it without any great regret.

CHAPTER IV

LASSALLE'S MANIFESTO AND ITS CONSEQUENCES

At last, in May, 1863, Lassalle published his Manifesto.* A few days earlier, on the occasion of the second anniversary of our Society, I had spoken against universal suffrage, arguing that the workers were not yet ripe for it. This action of mine had greatly shocked some of my friends, although my speech mightily pleased my future wife, who was among the audience.

The Manifesto by no means produced the effect upon the workers which had been anticipated by Lassalle and his friends. This was unavoidable, as the workers were still very backward in the economic as well as in the political sense. Liberty of trade, unrestricted movement, freedom of occu-

* " Open Letter to the Central Committee in regard to the convocation of a General German Labour Congress at Leipzig." This Manifesto is generally regarded as the starting-point of German Social Democracy.

pation and settlement, the abolition of passports, rights of association and meeting—these were demands which the workers understood, but of " productive associations with State help " they could make neither head nor tail. The idea of association or co-operation was only just evolving. Universal suffrage even was not regarded as indispensable by the majority of the workers.

It was precisely the Liberal Press which attacked Lassalle with the greatest vehemence, while the Conservative organs, such as the *Kreuzzeitung*, treated the matter more objectively, as they were not at all displeased by Lassalle's attacks on the Liberals. This Conservative support made us in Leipzig suspicious. But if we remember that even to-day, after more than fifty years of intensive efforts to enlighten the working classes as to their true interests, there are still millions of workers who follow the various bourgeois parties, it is not to be wondered at that the majority of the workers in the 'sixties regarded the new movement with sceptical eyes.

At Leipzig the effect of the Manifesto was a split in the Central Committee. The effect was almost everywhere the same ; Berlin completely failed to respond ; the movement gradually gained ground in Hamburg, and some half-dozen German cities, such as Hanover, Cassel, Düsseldorf, and Frankfort. Lassalle had hoped in a short time to obtain a hundred thousand members for a " General German Labour Union " to be reckoned with as a great political power. As a matter of fact a good many years were to elapse before the whole Socialist movement could number as many regular adherents. The Leipzig Committee, at a great public meeting, resigned its mandate, and a new Committee was elected to draw up a programme for the formation of a " General German Labour Union."

On the 16th of April Lassalle came to Leipzig. At a meeting of some four thousand people he expounded his ideas in a speech which later appeared in print as " The Labour Question." There were a good many Liberals present, who continually interrupted the speaker. In the subsequent discussion a leader of the Progressive Liberals protested against Lassalle's attacks on his party, and also against the proposal to form a special Labour party outside the Liberal party. Lassalle replied with great moderation, for he wanted for his movement not only the applause of the masses, but even more the assistance of influential leaders of the bourgeois parties, which he still hoped to win over to his side.

Lassalle's Manifesto and the formation of the General German Labour Union on the 23rd of May,

1863, led to violent disputes in the labour world, which lasted for many years. The exasperation increased with time, and more than once came to a head, resulting in blows and physical violence. The only good outcome of these disputes was that both factions made the greatest efforts to increase the number of their adherents, especially when a few years later the faction to which I belonged was converted to Socialism, but created its own organisation and continued to fight against the General Labour Union. But the amount of time, money, and energy expended upon internecine strife was wholly wasted, to the great satisfaction of our opponents.

In Leipzig Lassalleanism resulted in the amalgamation of the two Societies—my own and the Vorwärts Society—into a new Society known as the *Arbeiterbildungsverein* (Society for the Promotion of Knowledge among the Working Classes). Though the Society was in fact illegal, the Saxon Government took no steps against it. Our experience in this matter was one often since repeated— that all laws and measures of suppression miss fire and indeed become inoperative as soon as a movement proves to be according to nature and therefore unconquerable. I was elected vice-president of the new Society, a position which I held up to 1872, when I was condemned to detention in a fortress on account of attempted high treason against the German Empire.

Our Society received from the municipality an annual subvention of £75, but this was reduced to £10 when the Society became more Radical in its policy, in this instance following on the political development of its president—myself. The subvention was wholly withdrawn in 1869, when the Society, after a three-nights debate, resolved to adopt the programme of the German Social-Democratic party then just founded at Eisenach.

CHAPTER V

THE CONGRESS OF GERMAN WORKING-MEN'S SOCIETIES

THE number of Working-men's Societies (*Arbeiter-vereine*) had greatly increased, not only in Saxony but throughout the whole of Germany. Their objects were mostly educational ; some were just reading clubs. The energy and unity of purpose displayed by our adversaries, the Lassalleans, made us decide upon a closer union of our several societies. This union must necessarily be a very loose one, as we had no common and settled purpose as had the Lassalleans, a purpose for which they fought with self-sacrificing enthusiasm. The one thing the societies had in common was their hostility to the Lassalleans and their nominal exclusion of politics ; as a matter of actual fact the directors of most of these societies, or those who actually pulled the wires, did their best to make them serve party interests. All shades of the bourgeois party were represented, from the

Republican Democrats to Liberals of the Right—afterwards the National Liberal party. The members managed to rub along in spite of their political differences ; as for the " German question," the societies had adopted no definite line of action.

The Labour movement had spread to the West of Germany ; and on the occasion of a Labour Congress in Frankfort, in May, 1862, a violent dispute arose over the attitude of the working-classes. The barrister J. B. von Schweitzer—who was to play a very prominent part in the movement—advocated, evidently under the influence of Lassalle, the independent political organisation of the workers. A result of this dispute was the issue of a manifesto inviting the German Working-men's Societies to attend a Congress in Frankfort on the 7th of June, 1863. The Congress was attended by 110 delegates, representing 54 different societies established in 48 different towns. I was present as a delegate of the Workers' Improvement Society of Leipzig.

I give the first resolution in full because it expresses more clearly than a long disquisition the standpoint of the Congress :—

" The first Congress of German Working-men's Societies commences its proceedings with the proposition that in the opinion of the Congress it is the first duty of all Working-men's Societies

in general and of the working classes as a whole
to act in mutual unity in the prosecution of their
endeavours to improve the status of the working
class in the intellectual, political, civil, and
economic sphere, and to act in concord with
all those who work for the liberty and greatness
of the Fatherland and with all those who labour
for the improvement of mankind."

Although this resolution was obviously directed
against the Lassalleans, the name of Lassalle was
not mentioned, probably because no one believed
that the movement instituted by Lassalle had a
future before it.

Another resolution, which asked the societies to
have their members instructed in political economy
and constitutional theory, was rejected. To the
working-men of to-day such backwardness will
seem hardly credible. Other resolutions demanded
the liberation of labour from all reactionary fetters,
and the institution of workmen's banks, savings
banks, co-operative stores and co-operative productive associations, and co-operative societies, providing workshops fitted with power for the common
use, as the best means of promoting national
prosperity and the economic independence of the
workers. All these were the ideas of the Liberal
leader, Schulze-Delitzsch. The Congress recommended the co-operation of employers and

employed as the best means of accomplishing the above aims—a pious wish which was significant of the essentially lower-middle-class atmosphere of the meeting. Finally, invalidity and old-age insurance were recommended as capable of at least partially alleviating social distress. In the matter of organisation the Congress recommended provincial federation and monthly meetings of delegates, in order to promote the formation of new societies and to keep those already established in close touch with one another. The organisation finally adopted included an annual Congress, when the executive for the year would be elected, and a contribution of two thalers (six shillings) per society per annum. The means at the disposal of the executive were thus extremely modest—many societies failing to pay even the trifling subscription demanded. These anti-socialistic workers' societies were by no means eager to make sacrifices for the common good ; a comparison with the Lassalleans in this respect was by no means in their favour. The executive therefore applied to the *Nationalverein* for assistance, and obtained some £75 annually for a term of three years. Large employers of labour were privately approached, but gave very little ; antipathy for anything in the shape of working-men's clubs was already a bourgeois characteristic.

At Leipzig it was felt that the propaganda of the Lassalleans must be countered by energetic action. I was instructed to ask Schulze-Delitzsch to speak at one of our meetings. He consented, adding that we ought to be on our guard in Leipzig, as the workers of Saxony had evinced a leaning towards communistic and socialistic ideas as early as 1848. The meeting took place in January, 1864.

It was arranged that I was to welcome Schulze-Delitzsch, and was then to be elected chairman. I was unfortunate. When I opened the meeting some four thousand to five thousand people were present, and I broke down miserably in the middle of my speech, although I had carefully rehearsed it. I longed for the earth to swallow me. Some one else was elected chairman! I vowed never again to rehearse a speech, and I was right.

Schulze-Delitzsch was not a success. His speech was dry, and incapable of evoking enthusiasm. To many it was a disappointment; and it did nothing to stop the movement towards the Left.

We attempted to create a league of our societies in Saxony, and as it was as a matter of fact illegal to do so we applied to the Ministry for special permission. The Ministry gave the permission on the condition that the societies undertook not to meddle in political and social matters or public affairs of any kind. In response I proposed the following resolution at a public meeting :—

" The Working-men's Societies gratefully acknowledge the favour accorded them by Herr von Beust,* but prefer not to proceed with the matter."

A second resolution was put :—

" The delegates present urge the working-men of Saxony to work with all their might for the abolition of the existing laws of association." This resolution was objected to by the supervising police officer because it was " political." I protested, but had to desist, as he threatened to dissolve the meeting.

On the 31st of August, 1864, the telegraph informed the world that Ferdinand Lassalle was dead. He died at Geneva from a wound received in a duel. The resulting impression was profound. Most of his adversaries breathed freely again, as if relieved of an incubus ; they hoped his death would mean the end of the movement he had instigated. At first it seemed that they were right ; for the Labour Union, in spite of stupendous efforts, had only a few thousand members at the time of his death, and even these had begun to quarrel among themselves. Moreover, the man whom Las-

* Herr von Beust, the well-known Chancellor of Austria-Hungary of later years, was then Prime Minister of the kingdom of Saxony.

salle had appointed to be his successor was quite incapable of filling his place and entirely unfitted for the post. In a letter from a friend of mine, written at the time of Lassalle's death, it was suggested that we of the Working-men's Societies should not refuse the last honours to the dead; for although Lassalle was our opponent, his chief aim—the uplifting of the masses—was one with ours. Yet many a weary year had to elapse before this opinion became general.

The standing committee had decided upon Leipzig as the place of the next Congress. There was some opposition at first on account of the difficulties presented by the Saxon laws of association. Herr von Beust could make rain or sunshine as he pleased. To avoid the rain we decided to omit from the agenda the question of military service as being pre-eminently political. Finally, after much delay, von Beust gave the desired permission. The Congress was convened for the 23rd and 24th of October. I was elected chairman. The agenda was as follows :—

1. Right of free migration (abolition of the laws of settlement).

2. Co-operation : co-operative stores and co-operative production.

3. The standardisation of the courses of instruction provided by the societies.

4. Money grants for workers on the road (demanded especially by the young journeymen).

5. Old age insurance.

6. Life insurance.

7. Regulation of the labour market—*i.e.*, by means of Labour Exchanges.

8. Housing of the working classes.

9. Election of the executive.

Rather a long programme for two days of discussion ; but as the reports and resolutions were published beforehand we managed to go through with it, although not perhaps very thoroughly.

There were delegates from forty-seven societies and three provincial federations, and from several trades unions as well, some of them created for the occasion by the Lassalleans. There were also present Dr. Friedrich Albert Lange, of the Cooperative Society of Duisburg ; Dr. Max Hirsch, representing the Improvement Society of Magdeburg ; and as a guest a Conservative advocate of co-operation, Professor V. A. Huber.

The Congress saw some very turbulent scenes, the Lassalleans making some extremely violent speeches, to the disgust of the other delegates. Otherwise nothing of much note occurred. I was elected to the standing committee.

Here I will say a few words respecting Dr.

Lange. As members of the standing committee he and I were a good deal thrown together. He was one of the most lovable men I ever met, and conquered all hearts at the first meeting. He was a man of strong character, not influenced by threats. When he openly sided with the workers he became one of the outcasts of the industrial town of Duisburg. I was greatly indebted to him in the matter of the outcome of a newspaper quarrel— a paper insinuated that I was in the pay of Beust— in which he warmly defended me. After the war of 1866 he had to give up his post as Secretary to the Chamber of Commerce at Duisburg, and emigrated to Winterthur, in the canton of Zürich, in Switzerland, where he played a leading part in the agitation for a democratic reform of the reactionary Constitution of the canton. Later on he became a professor in the University of Zürich. In 1872 he was called to the University of Marburg by the Liberal Minister of Education of Prussia, Dr. Falk. There, in 1875, he died, at the early age of forty-seven. He was one of our best.

In the spring of 1865 the first German Women's Congress sat at Leipzig, and a General Association of German Women was founded. I was present at the debates as a guest. When the Leipzig Women's Educational Society asked us to lend them our rooms for a Sunday School for girls we willingly consented.

The year 1865, a year of prosperity, was also a year of many strikes for higher wages. At Leipzig the printers struck work. There were then no strike funds. An effort at conciliation on the part of a high official had failed, and Sonnemann * asked me to offer both sides the mediation of the standing committee. In spite of frequent consultations with both masters and men my efforts were not successful. But the attitude which a number of well-known Liberals had assumed toward the strikers prompted me to say, in No. 8 of the " Proceedings " of the standing committee, that the very men who had fawned on the people and protested their friendship for the workers had offered the most decided resistance to the demands of the workers. It was not therefore to be wondered at that even those workers who were most hostile to Lassalleanism should condemn those Liberals in the most unflattering terms.

* Proprietor of the *Frankfurter Zeitung.*

CHAPTER VI

THE CONGRESS AT STUTTGART: WILHELM LIEBKNECHT

THE third Congress of the Working-men's Societies was to be held at Stuttgart on the 3rd, 4th, and 5th of September, 1865. Sixty societies sent delegates, among whom were Hermann Greulich, Professor Eckhardt, Eduard Pfeiffer, a Stuttgart banker, and Professor Wundt, of Heidelberg, the famous physiologist and at present Professor of Physiological Psychology at the University of Leipzig. Greulich shortly afterwards went to Zürich, where he was, almost simultaneously with myself, converted to Socialism, and by the same teachers. Professor Eckhardt belonged to the extreme left wing of the Democratic party.

On the local committee there sat, besides Pfeiffer the banker, a barrister of the name of Hölder, who was later Minister of the Interior in Würtemburg. My duty was to report on the co-operative kitchen societies of Switzerland. My report was very meagre, and my printed speech in support of it very short. Max Hirsch contributed a report on the universal direct and equal suffrage, and put forward a resolution to the effect that the societies should devote all their energies to furthering it. Professor Wundt opposed the resolution, and put the previous question, in spite of general discontent. Finally the resolution was amended and accepted unanimously, only substituting the words "all German working-men" for "the societies."

Moritz Müller, a jewellery manufacturer, of Pforzheim, reported on the feminist question. In his printed report he recommended the complete social equality of women and men, the provision of continuation schools for women workers, and the formation of Working-Women's Societies. The debate on this resolution was the longest. The resolutions were carried, it being expressly understood that the social emancipation of women was to include women's suffrage.

The resolutions of the Stuttgart Congress were proofs of a further and a decisive movement towards the Left. On all questions of practical politics the so-called "Self-helpers" stood on a common platform. Our organisation was also somewhat improved. So long as the annual subscriptions were restricted to the absurd sum of six shillings from each society the standing committee was condemned to financial impotence. I proposed a subscription of one penny per member per annum, the president to be paid a salary of £45. My first proposal was voted by the Congress, and I was again elected to the standing committee.

The desire of the leaders of the bourgeois parties to obtain a preponderating influence over the societies was more in evidence than ever before. All felt that the German question was approaching a definite decision. The quarrels between Right and Left became more and more acrimonious. The antagonism between Prussia on the one hand and Austria and the smaller States of Germany on the other became more and more embittered. The German people was slowly working itself into a fever of excitement. This excitement was expressed even in the toast of the evening at the Congress banquet—which, by the way, was held in the very hall that forty-two years later, in August, 1907, witnessed the assembly of the first International Labour Congress held on German soil. While some of the delegates were covertly in favour of a Prussian hegemony, the Democrats spoke in favour of a radical solution of the problem, which we younger members understood to mean a German Republic, though the word was never uttered.

Just about this time a pamphlet had appeared, entitled "Germany's Liberation from Deepest

Disgrace," which openly advocated a German
Republic, which, of course, implied a revolution.
But the word " revolution " had then no terrors for
us. Memories of the revolution of 1848-9 had been
revived by the speeches and writings of active
participants therein. The possibilities of a successful revolution were then everywhere recognised.
Even Bismarck and Miquel had taken the con-
tingency into consideration. The opinions of
Lassalle, Marx, and Engels are plainly expressed
in their letters. The Memoirs of Prince Hohenlohe
prove that personages of very high standing in
South Germany had accustomed themselves to the
possibilities of a revolution. If those in high
places, why not those below?

The debates and resolutions of the Congress on
the rights of combination constituted a reply to
the debates on the same question in the Prussian
Parliament. Schulze-Delitzsch and Faucher—the
latter, a so-called political economist, seriously
undertook to prove, at a great public meeting in
Leipzig, that the social question would best be
solved by every workman learning book-keeping
by double entry and possessing a reliable time-
keeper in order to ensure making the best use of
his time—proposed certain amendments in the laws
of association, but significantly enough they did
not touch upon those clauses by which combina-

tions of workmen were dependent upon the permission of the police, nor on those prohibiting strikes. This greatly angered us, and the Conservative super-demagogue, Privy Councillor Wagener, exploited this Liberal timidity by proposing a motion which recommended, not only the abolition of all legal restrictions affecting the rights of the workers to form combinations, but also the formation on the part of the State of some sort of compulsory trades unions. The Conservatives at that period stopped at nothing that might have the effect of "dishing" the Liberals.

In 1865 and the beginning of 1866 it seemed likely that the contending parties of the Labour movement might unite. Thus, at a meeting in Mayence a motion was put that "as this division was contrary to the interests of labour in general, the members of the Working-men's Improvement Societies and those of the General German Labour Unions in the meeting assembled would do their utmost to bring about a union." A similar motion put to a meeting in Leipzig was defeated, but it was agreed that the parties should join forces in the fight for the universal, equal, direct, and secret suffrage. Another public meeting at Dresden, convened by the two Labour parties in conjunction, demanded a Constituent Assembly elected by universal suffrage, and the constitution of a universal militia under popular control for its protection and support. The same demands were made at a meeting in Berlin.

In August, 1865, Bismarck placed an interdict on the *Labour Gazette* of Coburg. One of those who fell a victim to his *régime* in Prussia, because he opposed his policy and denounced its true character to the workers, was Wilhelm Liebknecht.

Liebknecht was expelled from Prussia in July, 1865. He had returned in 1862, after thirteen years of exile, in consequence of the amnesty of 1860.*   He was invited by August Brass, an old revolutionary who had founded the *Norddeutsche Allgemeine Zeitung* † in Berlin, as a Greater German democratic journal, to take charge of the foreign news department. As Brass had been an ultra-Radical revolutionary Liebknecht trusted him absolutely. But in 1862, when Bismarck formed his Ministry, his suspicions were aroused. A manuscript was sent from the Minister with instructions to print it at once ; Liebknecht immediately gave notice and left. He then, having a wife and two children to support, made a living as a free-lance journalist, also giving lectures before meetings of workmen's clubs, in which he attacked the policy of Bismarck. He

* The occasion of the coronation of William I.
† Now a semi-official Government (Conservative) organ.

accused by J. B. von Schweitzer, then editor of the *Socialdemokrat*, of being one of Bismarck's hench-men. After his expulsion from Prussia he came to Leipzig, where I made his acquaintance ; having read in the newspapers of his activities and his expulsion from Prussia, I was greatly interested in his personality. He was then in his fortieth year, but had the vivacity and fire of a youth of twenty. We began a discussion on politics as soon as we were introduced. His vehemence and his condem-nation of the Liberal party, and of their leaders in particular, greatly startled me, though I myself was already aware that they were by no means impeccable. However, he was a man of the first class, and though he was rather abrupt in his manner we soon became friends.

Liebknecht was very welcome to us in Saxony. We had resolved to send travelling speakers about the country, but had no men suitable for the purpose. Liebknecht at once engaged in the work. He also lectured in the Workers' Improvement Societies, and his lectures drew more auditors than any. As well as lecturing he took classes in French and English. He gradually succeeded in making a modest competence, yet was obliged, as I learned later on, to sell many a choice volume from his library to the second-hand booksellers in order to provide adequate nursing for his wife, who was consumptive. But he made no parade of his straits ; indeed, those who met or listened to him gained the impression that his circumstances were quite satisfactory.

As I often accompanied him during his political tours, appearing on the same platform with him, our names were continually coupled, and the public regarded us as two inseparables. This was so far the case that when in the 'seventies I entered into partnership with a friend of mine, Issleib, I often received business letters addressed to not Issleib and Bebel but Liebknecht and Bebel, much to the amusement of my partner and myself.

Liebknecht's was the true fighter's temperament, supported by the unshakable optimism without which no great purpose can be achieved. No misfortune, whether private or affecting his party, ever for a moment dashed his spirits or disconcerted him. He could not be bluffed ; he could always find a way out of difficulties. The attacks of opponents he always met on the principle that the correct move is always *to go one better*. Brusque and inconsiderate to opponents, he was always helpful to friends and comrades, and always eager to smooth away their difficulties.

In his private life he was a good husband and father and devoted to his family. He was a true lover of Nature. A group of beautiful trees in otherwise unattractive surroundings would move him to enthusiasm and persuade him that the place was beautiful. He was unassuming in manner and simple in his tastes. An excellent soup which my young wife put in front of him soon after our marriage moved him to such enthusiasm that he did not forget it all his life. He was fond of a glass of beer or wine and a good cigar, but was never extravagant in such matters. When he appeared in a new suit—a thing that did not happen often —if I did not at once notice it and compliment him on the fact he would invariably, before many minutes had passed, call my attention to it, and ask for my approval. He was a man of iron, but his heart was the heart of a child. When he died, on the 7th of August, 1900, it was thirty-five years to a day since I had made his acquaintance.

In party matters Liebknecht had a way of meeting opposition to his plans with accomplished facts. At first I suffered from this propensity of his, for as a rule I had to swallow the brew of his mixing. In consequence of his deficiency in practical business ability others had to see to the execution of the measures he proposed. Finally, I summoned up courage to free myself from his somewhat dictatorial influence, but though we occasionally fell out the public never knew it, and our friendship was never long disturbed.

Much has been written of the extent to which
I was influenced by Liebknecht ; thus it has been
said that it was due to him that I became a Socialist
and a Marxist.   Liebknecht was fourteen years my
senior, and therefore had the advantage of me in
political experience ; he was also a University man,
which I was not.   He had lived for twelve years
in England, and there, in the course of intimate
intercourse with men like Marx and Engels, had
learned much.   I had never enjoyed such advan-
tages, so that it will be understood that Liebknecht
was bound to influence me greatly.   If he had not
done so it would have reflected on him, that he
was unable to influence me, or upon me, that I
was unable to learn from him.   But I should have
become a Socialist had I never known him, for
I was well on the road when we first met.   Having
continually to fight the Lassalleans, I had to read
their writings in order to grasp what it was that
they really wanted.   It was in this way that my
conversion was brought about.

My principle throughout life has been to abandon
any standpoint which I have taken up in respect
of any question so soon as I recognise it to be
untenable, and without reservation to adhere to
the newly won conviction and to stand up for it
manfully, both in public and private.   To go back
to the earliest instance of the kind, the attitude

of the Liberal leaders, in respect of their general policy as well as Labour questions, forced me to abandon my old position and to cross over to the Socialist camp. I did not suffer any particular pangs in so doing, and although I had to sacrifice many old and dear personal relations I took that as a natural consequence of my action. I have always, I venture to say, put causes before persons, and have never allowed myself to be diverted from my course by consideration of friends or relatives once that course was unavoidable in the interests of the cause I had embraced.

My friendship with Liebknecht certainly accelerated my conversion. It is the same with the story that Liebknecht was responsible for my becoming a Marxist. I listened to many a fine speech and lecture of his during those years. He lectured on trades unions, the English and French Revolutions, the German democratic movement, and political topics and questions of the day. When he referred to Marx and Lassalle he did so as a polemist; I never heard from him, to the best of my recollection, any coherent exposition of their economic theories. We both lacked time for private study, and the day's political battles left us no opportunity for private theoretical discussion. Further, by temperament Liebknecht was far more a politician than an exponent of theories. " High " politics were his preference.

No ; like most of us who then became Socialists, I went from Lassalle to Marx. Lassalle's writings were in our hands before we knew anything of Marx and Engels. My first pamphlet, " Our Times," which appeared towards the close of 1869, clearly proves Lassalle's influence on my political development. It was only then that I found leisure to study Marx's first volume—" Capital "—in prison. Five years earlier I had tried to study his " Political Economy," but had ignominiously failed ; over-work and the struggle for existence made it impossible for me inwardly to digest this difficult book. The Communist " Manifesto " and other writings became known to our party only late in the 'sixties and in the early 'seventies. The first work of Marx which I really understood and enjoyed was his " Inaugural Address " advocating the formation of the " International Working Men's Association " ; that was in 1865. In 1866 I became a member of the " International."

CHAPTER VII

THE CATASTROPHE OF 1866. THE WAR OF 1866 AND AFTER

THE working-classes, becoming more and more conscious of the highly unsatisfactory state of public affairs, were growing increasingly restive. They were unanimous in demanding a change ; but they had no leaders certain of their aims and able to inspire confidence, nor had they any powerful organisation capable of consolidating their forces, so that their revolutionary temper was completely inefficient in action. Never has a movement at heart so sound proved so ineffectual. All the meetings were packed to overflowing, and the more violent a speaker the more he was applauded.

At lectures given on the premises of our Society I as chairman was in the habit of adding some critical remarks and stating my own opinion. In this way differences of opinion were ventilated and difficulties explained. This method of thoroughly exploiting a lecture in the interests of the audience was extremely popular. But other methods were necessary in order to obtain definite results. As the federation of societies was illegal we were much hampered in our work; and as we had no newspaper the frequent personal interchange of opinion was all the more essential. We again applied to the Ministry for permission to form a provincial federation of our societies. The conditions imposed upon us were such as we could not accept; yet we decided to call a general meeting of all the societies and to draft a programme just as if there had been no legal prohibition. Although by order of the Director of Police we had effected certain modifications in our Society, it was shortly afterwards subjected to the laws of association—that is, treated as a political society, and therefore, of course, still more hampered in its work.

But all these questions were soon submerged by the political situation. In the spring of 1866 the antagonism between Prussia and Austria had come to a head. The gravity of the German question completely overshadowed all other questions and movements. The various sections of the Labour world agreed to act together. Numerous meetings were convened. The Saxon laws of association, which prohibited the federation of societies for political purposes, were completely disregarded, and a permanent co-operation of the Labour organisations was generally demanded. The parliamentary question was thenceforth the subject of the liveliest agitation among the working-classes. We asked for a Constituent Parliament for Germany as a whole (this, remember, was before the unification of Germany under the Empire), and the institution of a general "Citizen Army" for the protection of such Parliament. This demand was just then being put forward in all democratic circles as a matter of course; for it was said that a Parliament without such protection would always be subject to a *coup d'état*. Even the Liberal Schultze-Delitzsch declared, on the occasion of the meeting of the Association of German Rifle Clubs, in July, 1862: "The question of a permanent development of a liberal Constitution could not be solved under existing conditions, unless the National Army,* being, in fact, the nation armed, were to stand behind this Parliament." Later developments have proved the correctness of this opinion. A public meeting in Dresden even elected a delegation to lay its wishes and resolutions before the King. It was, of course, not received. But the ball had been set rolling, and it rolled in quite another direction from that generally anticipated.

To justify the attitude of my political friends

* The "National Army" was to be a militia controlled by Parliament.

and myself in respect of the war of 1866 I must give a brief summary of the events that led up to it. By the war, which was the culmination of the long-drawn-out diplomatic struggle between Prussia and Austria for the supremacy in German affairs, the German question was solved in a manner which so far no political party had worked for nor desired. Afterwards the great majority of the Liberals acquiesced in the new order of things ; as the political representatives of capitalism they expected therefrom a marked improvement in their material interests, and made their peace with the powers they had formerly opposed. But their defection did not in the least affect our standpoint.

By the death of Frederic VII., King of Denmark, in November, 1863, the Schleswig-Holstein question once more came to the fore. The people of those provinces refused to recognise the new King, Christian II., as their ruler, and decided in favour of Prince Frederic of Augustenburg. Thus the provinces once more became German, amidst universal approval. Denmark resisted, and the German Confederation decided on war. But this did not suit the schemes of Bismarck. He induced his " Crown Jurists " to declare the claims of the Prince of Augustenburg to be invalid, a decision which greatly incensed public opinion. People feared that Bismarck could not be trusted to settle the question in accordance with the wishes of the people of the affected provinces.

The executive of the *Nationalverein* published a manifesto asking all parishes, corporations, societies, and associations, and, lastly, all patriots, to provide men and arms and money to assist their German brothers of Schleswig-Holstein in the defence of their liberties. This manifesto was of course absolutely illegal, but there was no public prosecution. Public opinion was in sympathy with the lawbreakers. The branch Society of Schleswig-Holstein even admonished the youth of Germany to employ the probably short interval before the outbreak of hostilities in arming and drilling. It will be seen that the Liberal leaders of that time regarded the foundation of a people's army as a quite possible measure and one that need entail no great delay. Woe to the Social Democrat who should dare to publish a similar manifesto to-day! Here is progress with a vengeance!

From that time onwards many public meetings were convened all over Germany, with the object of advancing the cause of the Duchies. Thus at Leipzig a Labour meeting pledged itself to defend the honour, rights, and liberty of the Fatherland wherever threatened. But the people were against the annexation of the Duchies by Prussia. Finally, however, Bismarck had his way ; Prussia and Austria made war upon Denmark, and the latter was defeated and had to cede the provinces at stake, which were administered by the victorious Powers as a co-dominion. By this step Bismarck succeeded in widening the gulf between Austria and the German Confederation.

The new order in the Duchies could not last. The final settlement between Prussia and Austria, Bismarck considered, could only be attained by war, and he was systematically working to this end.

He tried to secure the neutrality of Napoleon by " dilatory negotiations," as he called them later on, and made arrangements by which Italy would attack Austria in the south while Prussia advanced upon the north. In the Parliament of the Confederation at Frankfort he brought in a motion to convene, at a date to be determined, an assembly elected by the whole of Germany by universal suffrage and the secret ballot. Austria would not assent, and the Governments of the other States and public opinion in general viewed Bismarck's proposal with the greatest distrust. Bismarck as a Radical reformer seemed too inconsistent with the unconstitutional Prussian Bismarck.

One consequence of Bismarck's policy was a split in the Liberal party. Some supported Bismarck and Prussia ; others opposed him. But when war became imminent the Liberals tried at least to ensure the neutrality of the smaller States.

In Saxony, on the contrary, the Liberals made their Government responsible for the eventual outbreak of war ; they demanded disarmament and alliance with Prussia. The municipality of Leipzig carried a resolution to the same effect, against which a public meeting convened by the Democrats and the Lassalleans, to which the Workers' Improvement Society acceded, protested. I proposed a strongly worded resolution condemning the Prussian policy, protesting against any hereditary central power in Germany, and recommending a Parliament elected by universal suffrage and secret ballot. My resolutions were carried unanimously. I spoke to the same purpose at a great democratic meeting at Frankfort, which was organised as a counter-demonstration to that of the members of the Frankfort Diet, who were favourable to the demands of Prussia. In my speech I protested against the idea of setting Prussia at the helm of Germany—Prussia which, save for the brief period from 1807 to 1810, when she was down in the dust, had never known a Liberal Government, and never would do so. The present war was due to Prussia, and if civil war should result the whole people ought to march against Prussia, the peacebreaker.

An executive was elected, of which I was a member, which drafted the following programme :—

1. The constitution and administration of the German States on democratic principles.

2. The voluntary confederation of the States.

3. A Federal Executive and Parliament, but neither a Prussian nor an Austrian predominance.

4. The Duchies to be self-governing.

5. Armed resistance against the Prussian war policy.

6. No cession of German territory to foreign Powers.

But before this programme could be published the war had commenced.

On the 10th of June the Standing Committee of the Working-men's Societies met at Mannheim to discuss the political conflict. The German question gave rise to heated debates. One member affirmed that a Prussian hegemony would greatly assist the industrial development of Germany, which another member denied. Finally it was decided that the societies should join the existing Populist (Radical) party, and accept the Frankfort programme, with the following amendment : " Every popular Government should promote the gradual adjustment of class antagonisms so far as consistent with individual liberty and the economic interests of the people as a whole ; and the material and moral improvement of the working-class is an interest common to all classes and an indispensable pillar of civic liberty."

As the political difficulties of the time had already greatly increased unemployment, it was resolved to ask the employers to work shorter hours in place of discharging workmen. The report of the treasurer was very unsatisfactory ; the *Labour Gazette*, we were told, would shortly expire for want of funds and supporters.

The war took a course much more favourable to Prussia than had been anticipated by many. In a few weeks Prussia was at the gate of Vienna. Austria was victorious in the south against Italy, but consented to a truce, which was concluded at Prague on the 22nd of August. The cession by Austria of Venice to Napoleon roused the German Liberals to a storm of indignation. Austria was accused of treason towards the Fatherland, a reproach which Prussia had to share. Had not Prussia made an alliance with Italy, a foreign Power, in order to crush a German State? Had not Bismarck opened negotiations with Klapka, the revolutionary general of Hungary, with a view to inciting Hungary to rise against Austria? Did not Bismarck stretch out a protecting hand over the Saxon Liberals, who had voted a resolution in favour of the annexation of Saxony by Prussia, by stipulating, in the treaty of peace, for an amnesty for all concerned in such actions? But these same Liberals did their utmost in 1870 to secure the conviction of Liebknecht and myself for high treason !

Liebknecht and I have often in later years been asked what we thought would have happened had Austria been victorious. It is in all truth sad enough that there was only that alternative—that to side with the one Power meant to side against the other—but that could not be helped. My personal opinion is that for a people which is not free defeat is rather favourable than otherwise to its internal development. Victories result in a Government the reverse of democratic in type, haughty and exacting in quality, while reverses force the Government to approach the people and to win its goodwill. Thus it was in Prussia after 1806-7, in Austria after 1866, in France after 1870, and in Russia after the Japanese victories of 1904. The Russian Revolution would never have broken out except for the Russian losses. A few victories on the part of the Tsar's troops would have made it impossible for years to come. And although the Revolution failed, old Russia disappeared for ever just as old Prussia disappeared after 1847-9. On the other hand, history tells us that when the peoples of Prussia had, at the cost of enormous sacrifices of blood and treasure, defeated the first Napoleon's foreign tyranny and saved the dynasty from ignominy, the dynasty proceeded to forget all the fine promises it had made the people in the hour of danger. It was only in 1848 that the people at last obtained the payment of what had been justly due to it for decades. And did not Bismarck at a later date refuse all really Liberal demands in the North German Diet, acting, indeed, like a dictator? Had Prussia been defeated, would not the ministry of Bismarck and the domination of the Junker party, which oppresses Germany to this day, have been swept away together? The Austrian Government would never, even in the event of victory, have been as strong as the Prussian Government became. Austria was, and is still, a weak State because of its structure; the reverse is true of Prussia. But the Government of a strong State is much more dangerous to its democratic development. In no democratic State is there what is called a strong Government. As against the people it is powerless. If victorious, the Austrian Government would probably have resorted to reactionary measures. It would in that case have found ranged against it, not only the whole Prussian people but also a great part of the rest of Germany and even of its own population. A revolution against Austria would have had very great chances of success, in which case the unification of Germany on a democratic basis would have been possible. But the victory of Prussia put an end to these speculations. It also had another result. The exclusion of German Austria from the Confederation condemned millions of Germans to an almost hopeless condition. Our "patriots" fall into a frenzy of nationalistic fury if a German is badly treated anywhere abroad ; but they do not protest against the spiritual assassination, if I may so call it, of the ten millions of Germans in Austria.

I learned later on that the great personalities of our movement had discussed these questions before 1866. Thus Lassalle wrote to Marx in June, 1859 : "In a war against France I do see a misfortune—only if it be a popular war. In an unpopular campaign I foresee an immense advantage to the Revolution. A victory over France would damage the revolutionary idea immensely. It is still the fact that France, in spite of all her Napoleons, stands for revolution, and that a defeat of France means a defeat of the revolution." And in March, 1860, Lassalle wrote to Engels : " I hope I was not misunderstood when I wrote last year in my pamphlet on the Italian war (1859) that I most ardently desired a war between Prussia and Napoleon. I desired it only on condition that the war should be conducted by the Government and should be unpopular with the people—indeed, as much hated by the people as is possible. Then and only then such a war would be a piece of the greatest good luck." In a lecture given in October, 1862, he stated : " And finally the existence of the Germans is not so precarious that a defeat of their Governments would really jeopardise the national existence. If you, gentlemen, will consider history intelligently and scrupulously, you will see that the works achieved by our people are so vast and significant, we broke so much new ground, and are responsible for so much intellectual progress that our existence is beyond a doubt both necessary and inevitable. If we have to undertake a great external war, some of our States—Prussia, Bavaria, or Saxony—may be destroyed, but even as the phœnix from its ashes there would arise, indestructible, that which alone matters—the German people."

The results of the war seemed likely to benefit us by an unexpected success. Liebknecht came to my workshop beaming with delight one day to inform me that he had just bought a newspaper which had been abandoned by the Liberals on account of its increasing deficit. He had even undertaken to pay some £120 of debts. I was very greatly perturbed, for we had not a penny in our chest, and it was quite hopeless, under the circumstances, to think of developing the paper. Moreover, we had to reckon with the Prussian occupation. But Liebknecht tried to console me. The proprietor did not ask for cash down, and we could easily provide for the necessary expenses. Liebknecht was overjoyed at the idea of having a paper in which he could write whatever he liked. And that he did with a vengeance, as though he, and not Prussia, were the master. His pleasure was not of long duration. His paper was suppressed, and I was not at all sorry ; but I did not tell him so. We were saved from considerable embarrassments ; for Liebknecht's scheme for selling five thousand shares at a thaler (three shillings) apiece to the German Working-men's Societies would certainly have been a total failure.

One consequence of the war was the rise of the North German Confederation, in which Prussia the giant dominated the other lesser States. As the convocation of a North German Diet elected by universal suffrage became probable, we found ourselves in need of a more permanent political organisation and a programme around which the new party could rally. The programme could not be openly Social-Democratic, as some of the leading elements of the party were antagonistic, and some of the workers' unions were still rather backward in political matters. It was essential to avoid a split at this stage of developments, and having regard to the profoundly excited condition of large portions of the bourgeois classes, due to the events of the war and the disintegration of Germany into three parts (North Germany, South Germany, and Austria), it was important to concentrate all our energies on the democratisation of Germany.

We therefore called a meeting at Chemnitz, attended by the members of the General German Labour Union, for the purpose of establishing the new Democratic party. The following programme was voted :—

DEMANDS OF DEMOCRACY.

1. Unrestricted right of the people to determine its own form of government. Universal, equal, and direct suffrage by secret ballot in all branches of public life (Parliament, the Diets of the several States, and local government bodies). Militia in place of standing armies. A Parliament with complete sovereignty, and especially the right to determine on peace and war.

2. The unification of Germany under democratic government. No "Little Germany" under a Prussian hegemony ; no Prussia augmented by annexations ; no Greater Germany under Austrian hegemony ; no Triad State (South, North, and

Austria). These and other similar " dynastic-particularist " experiments, which would inevitably result in loss of liberty, disintegration, and foreign interference, are to be opposed to the utmost by the Democratic party.

3. Abolition of all privileges of birth, caste, and religion.

4. The improvement of the people in a physical, intellectual, and moral sense. Secularisation of schools, separation of Church and State. The transformation of the Elementary Schools into a public institution supported by the State, with gratuitous instruction. Free Continuation Schools.

5. The furtherance of the commonweal and the liberation of labour and labourers from all oppression and restriction. Improvement of the condition of the working classes, liberty of settlement, freedom of occupation, rights of universal German citizenship, and the assistance and promotion of co-operation, especially productive co-operation, in order to allay the antagonism of capital and labour.

6. Local self-government.

7. The fostering of an increased respect for the law among the people by means of independent courts and the jury system, especially in political and Press trials, with public and oral procedure.

8. The promotion of the political and social education of the people by means of a free Press,

the right of meeting and association, and the right of coalition.

Certainly this programme left nothing to be desired on the score of Radicalism. Although the members of the General German Labour Union (the Socialists) accepted it they did not join the party.

The imminence of the elections to the North German Diet necessitated an intensive organisation and propaganda, which imposed many sacrifices upon all of us. The Social-Democratic propagandists are often pilloried by their bourgeois opponents as people who thrive on the miserable earnings of the working-man. While this charge had never any substratum of truth in it, at the time of which I write it was particularly absurd. A really stupendous amount of enthusiasm, perseverance, and self-sacrifice was requisite in those who undertook the work of agitation. The agitator had to content himself with the repayment of his bare out-of-pocket expenses, and those he had to keep as low as possible. Any invitation from a political friend who offered house-room was accepted as a matter of course, although these friends were mostly poor devils whose accommodation was of the most modest description. Our experiences were sometimes unusual. More than once I had to sleep in the same room as man

and wife ; once it happened that the household
cat was delivered of kittens under the sofa which
served me as bed, to the accompaniment of much
mewing and lamenting. Another time a friend and
I were quartered in the garret where our host,
who was a weaver, kept his yarn. When I was
awakened in the morning by the sun shining on
my face I discovered myself lying on a mass of
yellow yarn, while my friend's pillow was a heap
of scarlet yarn. Similar experiences were the lot
of all who then and later worked as agitators for
the party. Liebknecht, too, was very active, but
his work was unexpectedly interrupted. Trusting
to the amnesty granted in Prussia after the war,
he went to Berlin to deliver a lecture, when he
was arrested and condemned to three months' imprisonment. He was treated as a common
criminal ; for instance, he had no light after
6 p.m., which was a great hardship.

The elections took place in February, 1867.
As our means were restricted we put up only three
candidates, in divisions where our organisation was
strongest. I was elected in Glauchau-Meerane
and a barrister friend in Zwickau-Crimmitschau ;
Liebknecht was defeated. I had four opponents,
and was victorious in the second ballot by 7,922
votes against 4,281.

Already many of the elections were fought by

very dishonest means. Travelling by rail I had often to listen to violent abuse. On one occasion a traveller in the next compartment stated that I had promised the weavers double wages and an eight-hour day if I was elected. Incensed by these lies and his abuse of me, I went up to the man and asked him whether he had these facts from Bebel himself. When he said yes I called him an impudent liar, and gave my name as he became offensive. This silenced him, and amid the jeers and laughter of his fellow-travellers he hurriedly left the carriage at the next station.

There was a second election in 1867. Four of us were elected, including Liebknecht. The Lassalleans were successful in three divisions, and another branch of the General German Labour Union which had seceded from the Lassalleans won one election and later on a second. There were thus altogether nine of us Labour members.

CHAPTER VIII

PROGRESS OF THE ASSOCIATION OF GERMAN WORKERS' SOCIETIES. PRIVATE AFFAIRS

THE political events of the year 1866 had been disastrous to our societies. We had no money, our newspaper had ceased publication, two others which we started had fared no better, and until a third was founded—the *Democratic Weekly*, edited by Liebknecht—we had no organ by which we could express our views and enlighten our adherents in political and social matters, a task of the greatest importance, nor any defence against the attacks of our opponents. We had to make the greater sacrifices to keep the paper going, but we did so willingly, for the paper was our most effective weapon. I was, of course, a frequent contributor.

I was dissatisfied with the weakness of our executive. In a letter I protested against the continued endeavour to keep the societies divorced from politics, and proposed to get into touch with the "International," and to improve our organisa-

tion in view of the evident hostility of the North
German Confederation to the cause of Labour.

Our fourth Congress sat on the 6th and 7th of
October, at Jena, and at last accepted my proposals
as to organisation, which I had pressed on them
for years. The president of the Association for
the year was to be elected by the Congress, while
the Society to which the president belonged was
to elect an executive of six, its domicile becoming
the headquarters of the Association for the time
being. The president was to receive 300 thalers
(about £45) for his services. In addition to the
executive sixteen " confidential agents " were to be
elected for the whole of Germany, to control the
financial business of the executive and advise it in
important matters. I was elected president by
nineteen votes out of thirty-three, so that Leipzig
became our headquarters. The " new policy " had
gained the day, and at last we had obtained what
I had striven for : the Association was at last in
the way of efficiency.

This was the first German Labour Congress to
demand an Employers' Liability Act. The occasion
of the demand was a great disaster in a coalpit,
in which 101 miners had been killed. Our
demand was granted in 1872 by an Imperial Act,
which did not, however, satisfy us.

The new organisation put a new spirit into the

Association. Our first business was to awaken the majority of the societies from their indifference, and stimulate them to energetic action. To this end we had to set them tasks worthy of exertion. Every number of our paper was headed by some manifesto claiming the activities of the societies for the most varied business. Success was almost immediate. The societies awoke to life, and their contributions were paid with quite unknown regularity. The business of the executive had almost entirely to be discharged by myself ; I was president, secretary, and treasurer all in one. The business to be transacted with the Societies increased enormously ; from 253 inquiries and 543 replies in 1867-8 to 907 inquiries and 4,484 replies in 1868-9, the replies mostly taking the form of newspapers and reading matter, but all the rest were letters, written by my own hand, and frequently very long letters.

I had also to preside at the meetings of the executive. I was still president of the Workers' Improvement Society ; I was a member of the North German Diet, and of the Customs' Diet also. I undertook numerous journeys in the interest of the party propaganda, and was a permanent contributor to the *Democratic Weekly*, for which I wrote the "Labour column" in its entirety. It will be understood that in consequence of so much work I neglected my young wife and my small business in the most inexcusable manner, so that financially I was in a very bad way, and very often could hardly see my way ahead. It came to this for most of us : either we had to give up active politics or go out of business. If our opponents to this day say that there is, for instance, not one genuine workman among the members of the Social-Democratic party in the Reichstag, this is very easily explained : any workman who openly works for Social-Democracy is instantly dismissed. Either he keeps a quiet tongue or the party, requiring agitators, editors, and other active workers, has to provide for him. It is still worse for men who are in trade for themselves. Our opponents often complain of the terrorism of the Social-Democratic party. But that is rank hypocrisy. Their own terrorism is worse. I have seen many a good friend slowly bled to death by the terrorism of his political adversaries. It is easy to understand why we have so many cigar and tobacco dealers and restaurant keepers among our Members of Parliament ; they had to take to these callings because they had been *dismissed by their employers on account of their political ideas*, and these were almost the only trades in which their party friends could assist them by their custom. I myself, in the course of the twenty-five years during which I was in business, had often to suffer loss of custom and damage by the conflict of public and private interests.

Repeatedly friends of mine who did not meddle with politics and did not understand my work for the Labour movement told me I was a silly fellow to sacrifice myself for the working-people. If I would only devote myself to local politics and the interests of the middle classes, I should certainly prosper and might even eventually become an alderman. I used to laugh at this ; my ambitions did not lie in that direction.

How I contrived to get through all this work— the years 1867-72 were the most laborious of my life—may be a riddle to many. To a certain extent it was a riddle to me, for I had to struggle with poor health as well as other disadvantages. I was of small stature, hollow-cheeked, and pale. Friends of my wife who were guests at our wedding were wont to say, " Poor dear, she'll not have him for long ! "

But as luck had it they were mistaken.

*　　　*　　　*　　　*　　　*

Here I may conveniently insert some account of my private affairs. To the man who has in his public life to encounter a host of enemies the choice of the woman who is to share his life is by no means a matter of indifference. She may be a helpmate and support him in his aims through life, or she may be a dead weight and a hindrance. I am happy to be able to say that my wife was one of the former category. She was the daughter of a railway navvy who died before we met. She worked in a millinery shop. We became engaged in 1864, shortly before the death of her good mother, and were married in the spring of 1866. I never had cause to regret it ; I could not have found a more lovable, loving, and self-sacrificing wife. Whatever I have achieved has been due to her ready help and indefatigable care. And before the sun of quieter times shone upon us we had to pass through many days, months, and years of trouble. A daughter who was born to us in January, 1869, was a source of consolation and happiness in many a dark hour.

My share in the Labour movement and my engagement made a permanent settlement in Leipzig desirable. Although Saxony had in 1863 established liberty of trades and crafts, every non-Saxon was regarded as a foreigner and had to be " naturalized " before setting up in business on his own account. But this cost money, some £7 10s., including the freedom (citizenship) of the city of Leipzig. From home I could count on about £50. My master having dismissed me, I was obliged to set up for myself. I went to Wetzlar to get together as much ready money as possible, and hired a workshop in Leipzig, in a house that had been transformed into business premises, having previously been a stables. It was an extremely uncomfortable place, not even boasting a fireplace, and for want of means we had to use it as a dwelling; on winter nights I was miserably cold. As I could not afford to pay for " naturalization " I first used the name of a friend of mine, becoming " naturalized " on borrowed money only when I married. I began business in a very small way, with only one apprentice. A few months later I was able to engage a journeyman. I encountered all the difficulties that beset the small business. I had to give long credit, yet I had to provide cash for wages and household expenses. I had to sell my work to a middleman for little more than the cost price. Moreover, I lost on the paper money with which the small German States were flooding the country. Eventually my public work brought me into notoriety with the employers, and I was boycotted. Had I not succeeded in building up a certain trade with other towns (I made door and window handles of buffalo horn), I must have gone bankrupt. Business went from bad to worse in the years of the war, 1870-1, when trade came to a standstill. My wife wrote to me while I was

in prison with Liebknecht during the time of my
trial for high treason that for 102 days not an
article had been sold, while the man and apprentice had to be paid their weekly wages. But
things improved during the boom that followed the
war, which lasted till 1874 ; I then got more orders
than I could execute. When in the spring of 1872
Liebknecht and I began to serve our sentences—
twenty-two months' detention in a fortress, and in
my case nine months of prison to follow—I was
able to leave the business to my wife, who employed
a foreman, six workmen, and two apprentices.
Though my wife did her best she did not coin
money. I did the necessary correspondence from
the fortress or prison. Another crisis followed
when the boom collapsed, when my specialities
were put on the market at prices I could not compete with, made by machinery. I was thinking of
giving up business in order to become an official
of the party, when by chance I met a political
friend, Ferdinand Issleib, who in addition to the
necessary business experience had sufficient means
to set up a small factory with steam power. We
became partners and soon acquired a good reputation. It was now my duty to visit the customers
and solicit orders—in short, to act as "traveller"—
an occupation which at a later date, when the law
against Socialism was introduced, enabled me to

do the party valuable service. When I was expelled from Leipzig and once more had to go to prison, we dissolved the partnership and I became simply the traveller for the business. Finally, in 1889, I gave up this position to devote my whole time to writing.

It is curious to note that most people had formed a mental picture of my person very different from the reality. My partner resembled this picture exactly. He was a big, strong man, with red hair, and a red beard which swept his breast. When any one came to the office to see me who had not met me before he would begin by addressing my partner. It often happened that I would enter a railway carriage unrecognised by my fellow-travellers, and find myself listening to the most blood-curdling stories about myself. In most circles I was regarded as a sort of Robin Hood, and a man who wanted to subvert the whole social order. People I met in the ordinary way of society were often heard to exclaim : " Why, this Bebel is quite a respectable sort ! " This was intended as a compliment.

CHAPTER IX

THE CONGRESS AT NUREMBERG

In July, 1867, after lengthy negotiations, a treaty was concluded between Prussia and the South German States creating the so-called Customs Diet, an assembly to consider questions relating to the Customs duties and the indirect taxation common to both halves of Germany. This assembly was to be composed of the members of the North German Diet and specially elected deputies from South Germany. The South German People's party, which demanded full admission to the North German Confederation, a demand which Bismarck refused to consider, decided to abstain from voting, in spite of our urgent advice. However, we succeeded in getting some South German Democrats elected to the Diet.

In Bavaria and Wurtemburg the Workers' Unions were agitating for the introduction of the militia system. The Wurtemburg Government had consented to reduce the term of military service to nineteen months only, while in Bavaria the term was only nine months. But this success was annulled by the Franco-German War and the entrance of the South German States into the Confederation.

We of the executive were convinced that the political divergence of the two parties in the Association of Workers' Societies ought not to continue. Having obtained the supreme power since the last Congress, I was anxious to wield it to the best advantage. It was essential that a definite programme should be adopted, whatever the consequences to the unity of the League. We therefore asked Robert Schweigel—who was then co-editor with Liebknecht of the *Democratic Weekly*—to prepare a draft programme, on the same basis as that of the International Working Men's Association, and to report on it at the next Congress.

As soon as it became known that we proposed to lay a programme before the next Congress, there was great excitement among those societies which were directed by the Liberals. We were assailed by the Liberal Press of both north and south. I received many letters of protest and warning, prophesying defeat. I answered that social reform could not be separated from politics ; they were, in fact, complementary. In his own interests the working-man ought to be a Democrat. The nebulous condition that then obtained must not continue. In another letter I added that if the majority of the societies should reject a Social-Democratic programme, the executive and the majority of the members of the Saxon societies would probably secede from the League.

To prevent a split I started a vigorous campaign, writing to all those whom we thought favourable to our plan. But as I myself was not quite certain of the position taken by some of the members of the Association, I received a certain number of rebuffs. This did not, however, affect the final result.

Meanwhile Moritz Müller, of Pforzheim, had recommended the formation of trades unions, and initiated a campaign whose object was to exclude professors and doctors (that is, University men) from the leading positions in the movement. I wrote agreeing with him. The printers and cigarmakers had already followed the example of the English workers, and the bootmakers of Leipzig and bookbinders of Dresden were about to follow suit. I also was of opinion that the workers should choose their leaders from their own ranks; we knew from experience that the doctors and professors were of no use to us.

J. E. Becker, the president of the German branch of the "International" at Geneva, wrote to me asking if we would join the "International." I replied that for the present it was impracticable, but promised to ask the Congress to declare itself in agreement with the aims and objects of the "International" and to establish the closest relations with it. At the same time I asked him to send a delegate to Nuremberg.

As had been expected, the Congress, which sat from the 5th to the 7th of September, was very well attended ; there were 155 delegates from 93 societies. As invited guests there were present : Eccarius, from London, representing the General Council of the "International" ; two delegates from the Vienna Workers' Improvement Society ; two delegates from Swiss societies ; Dr. Ladendorf, from Zurich, a revolutionist who had served a term of penal servitude in Germany, from the German Republican Society ; a delegate from the German branch of the "International" in Geneva ; one from the French branch ; two delegates from the executive of the German People's party (Democratic) ; a member of the General German Labour Union—the Lassallean Society—was also present, though not officially. He was, so to speak, the first swallow that ventured to nest with us ; and his action was a crime in the eyes of the leader of the Lassalleans, J. B. von Schweitzer.

The Congress held its meetings in the great

historic hall of the municipality, which the Town
Council had lent us in the hope that the Liberals
would be victorious.   I opened the meeting with
a speech of welcome to the foreign delegates, and
proceeded to the election of a chairman.   Out of
ninety-four votes I received sixty-nine.   From that
moment the final decision was no longer in doubt.
The two vice-chairmen elected were also of our
party ; our opponents were defeated all along
the line.   They tried to move the previous question, but with shouts of " No compromise ! "
the order of the day was voted by a great
majority.

The debates of the Congress shaped excellently ;
it was really one of the finest meetings I ever took
part in.   As reporter of the general business of
the Association I was able to say that the new
organisation had worked admirably and that the
Association was in a splendid position compared
with former times.   The associated societies had
now 13,000 members.   The debate on the programme was followed with breathless interest.   The
final result of the voting was 69 societies with
69 votes for the programme and 32 with 46 votes
against.   The minority protested, left the hall, and
took no further part in the debates.   Their attempt
to form a new organisation, under the title of " The
Labour Alliance," was unsuccessful.   The societies

lost all political significance and became appendages of the several Liberal parties.

Our programme was as follows :—

" The Fifth Congress of German Workers' Societies in session at Nuremburg declares its adhesion to the programme of the International Working Men's Association on the following points :—

" 1. The emancipation of the working-classes must be effected by those classes themselves. The struggle for the emancipation of the working-classes is not a struggle for class privileges and monopolies, but for equal rights and equal duties and the abolition of all class-domination.

" 2. The economic dependence of the worker on the monopolists of the instruments of labour is at the root of every kind of servitude, social misery, intellectual degradation, and political dependence.

" 3. Political liberty is the indispensable instrument for the establishment of the economic emancipation of the working-classes. The social question is therefore inseparable from the political question, its solution depends on it, and is possible only in a democratic State.

" Further, in consideration of the fact that all attempts in the direction of the economic emancipation of the workers have so far been wrecked by the **want** of solidarity between the many branches of labour in the same country and the non-existence of a fraternal bond of union between the working-classes of the several countries:

"And that the emancipation of labour is not a local or national but a social problem common to all countries with modern societies, the solution of which depends upon the practical and theoretical co-operation of the more progressive nations:

"Be it resolved by the Fifth Congress of German Workers' Societies to adopt the aims of the International Working Men's Association."

These resolutions left no doubt as to the attitude assumed by our societies. Yet the General Meeting of the People's party (Democratic), which was called a few days later, behaved as if nothing had really happened; it even declared its agreement with the Nuremburg resolutions. In this they gave proof of a degree of discernment which was conspicuous by its absence among our latter-day Radicals. It was more especially Sonnemann who tried at all costs to prevent the secession of the Workers' Societies from the People's party.

By the secession of the minority the agenda of the Congress broke down, as several of the reporters on questions to be discussed were among the seceders. Sonnemann reported on the foundation of the Old Age Pensions Funds under State control. But his proposals were rejected, especially on the grounds that State control would tend to make the workers unconsciously Conservative with regard to the existing State, which was quite unworthy of confidence ; a conviction shared by Bismarck, who declared later that small pensions for the worker were the best means of reconciling him with the existing order of the State—a conviction underlying his invalidity and old age insurance laws. Other resolutions recommended the formation of old age and sickness funds by centralised trades unions.

I was again elected president by fifty-seven votes out of fifty-nine, so that Leipzig remained our headquarters for another year.

The Commission elected to report on the management of the executive gave us high praise. (The remuneration for the work done was something under £8.) All books and papers were found to be in the best possible order, calling for the warmest possible thanks.

I was attacked in the Opposition Press for trying to pervert the workers by a "social-communistic programme." I replied that the words "Socialist" and "Socialism" had now grown too tame. The workers had gradually discovered that Socialism was, after all, nothing so terrible ; the word "communism" had to be employed to terrify the Philistines.

The resolutions of the Nuremburg Congress
created a new situation. It was impossible for
Schweitzer any longer to make us suspect by the
Lassallean party and to brand us in his *Socialdemokrat* as a lower-middle-class bourgeois party.
It could no longer be contested that the Saxon
People's party and the League of Workers' Societies
were Socialist parties standing on the same platform as the " International."

Our poor financial position was still our most
serious weakness. Although we had ten thousand
members, a penny per member per year did not
go far.

Our *Democratic Weekly* required a considerable
subsidy. We had started it with some ten thalers
(thirty shillings) in our pockets. Many party
papers were founded on a very similar basis ; they
were really bankrupt when their first numbers came
out. But the enthusiasm and willingness to make
any sacrifices for such papers were unlimited. Of
course, the editors had to be content with very
little remuneration. The present generation can
hardly conceive of the wretched poverty of our
conditions, or the amount of unpaid work which
was demanded of us. Thus Liebknecht, as editor
of the *Democratic Weekly*, received some £6
monthly, and later, as editor of the tri-weekly
Volksstaat (the *People's State*), some £9 15s.   I

contributed the labour column of the former paper without receiving any remuneration, and only received about 36s. monthly for the distribution of the paper, out of which I had to provide an office ! When the war of 1870 broke out I even chose to forego this small payment. Rises in salary were quite unknown. Thus when *Vorwärts,* the successor of the *Volksstaat,* was suppressed, in 1878, Liebknecht was receiving the same salary as nine years earlier. As far as financial conditions go, we are to-day really a " bourgeois " party as compared with the party of those days.

But our party had always wonderfully good luck, which made me tell my friends : " If there is a God, He seems to be very fond of Social-Democracy ; for our extremity is always His opportunity." This was seen in the matter I am about to relate. I was just confiding our money difficulties to a friend of mine when the postman brought me a registered letter. Opening it, I found it came from Dr. Ladenburg, of Zurich, who informed me that from funds entrusted to him and his friends, the so-called " Revolutionary Fund," I was to receive 3,000 francs (£120) in three instalments, concerning the application of which I was to account to him. More than once this " Revolutionary Fund " came to our rescue. The source dried up when we

no longer saw eye to eye with Ladenburg in respect
of the resolutions of the International Labour Congress at Basle, as affecting questions of land reform,
and further differed from him in our attitude
towards the war of 1870.

CHAPTER X

THE TRADES UNION MOVEMENT

I SHALL write of the Trades Union movement only in so far as I helped to bring it into the world. The year 1868 may be given as the year of the birth of German trade unionism, although organisations of workers similar to the unions existed before that date, such as a Union of Cigar-makers and a Printers' Union. In 1865, a year of prosperity, there were numerous strikes; but in most of these the workers had to give in for want of organised resistance and funds. This taught them the necessity of both.

So far the political leaders had done little for trades unionism. It was Liebknecht, with his lectures on English trades unionism, who did most to clear the way. We of the executive considered the matter, but pressure of work prevented us from taking any active steps.

In the summer of 1868 Max Hirsch went to England to study the English unions. He published an account of his experiences in the Berlin

Volkszeitung, and Schweitzer, of the *Socialdemo-krat*, who was of opinion that Hirsch wanted to establish unions simply in order to keep the workers within the fold of the Progressive (Liberal) party, endeavoured to forestall him. He proposed, at a meeting of the General German Labour Union, to convene a General Congress of German Workers for the purpose of forming trade unions. His proposals, however, were rejected. We members of the Association of Workers' Societies had voted without debate, at the Nuremburg Congress, for the formation of unions. Schweitzer none the less set to work, and a Congress of 206 delegates at Berlin, representing 190,000 workers, decided on the formation of so-called *Arbeiterschaften* (workers' associations), under a central executive, the direction of which remained entirely in the hands of Schweitzer. He would not allow the slightest degree of independence to any part of the movement. The organisation was condemned root and branch by Marx, on whose support Schweitzer had counted. Soon afterwards Schweitzer tried to modify this organisation and to amalgamate it with the General German Labour Union. The Lassalleans generally were hostile to trades unionism. They regarded it merely as a means to an end, the end being to get the unions into the party and then dissolve them.

The standing committee at Leipzig immediately got to work on a schedule of standard rules for trades associations. I was the author of these rules. As soon as prepared they were sent out to all the societies with a recommendation to proceed forthwith to the foundation of " International Trades Associations," for such was the title we had decided upon. I spoke in support of the measure at numerous meetings. The word " International " was a little ambitious, for we could hardly hope to extend our organisation beyond the German-speaking countries. But we chose the title as a demonstration of our purpose. A number of similar associations were indeed formed, such as the International Trade Association of factory hands and other manual labourers, of masons and carpenters, metal-workers, wood-workers, tailors, furriers, and capmakers, bootmakers, bookbinders, miners, and iron-workers.

It cannot be denied that while the political movement' was greatly impeded by dissensions the trades union movement suffered even more. None of the political fractions of the Labour party would renounce the formation of its own special union, hoping thereby to obtain an accretion of power.

At Leipzig we did our best to prevent dissension within the movement, and with this object called

a meeting in October, 1868, in conjunction with
the members of the General German Labour Union.
It was resolved at this meeting to promote with
energy the formation of trades unions, and a committee was elected to take the requisite steps.
Liebknecht and I were on this committee, together
with members of the General Union. We invited
members of all trades to appear before the committee in order to discuss the organisation of
unions. It was resolved to call a joint general
meeting for the purpose of amalgamation, and that
pending such amalgamation both bodies should
agree to give mutual assistance, especially in respect
of finances, but that neither should under any
circumstances enter into relations with the
" Hirsch-Duncker Unions," " which, founded by the
enemies of labour, had no other aim than to prevent
the adequate organisation of labour, and to degrade
the workers into instruments of the bourgeoisie."

But our advances were rejected by the other
side. Schweitzer and his General Union dissented
from our proposals. The extreme Lassalleans were
even more hostile. They regarded the creation
of trades unions as a violation of Lassalle's principles and organisations, and these were sacrosanct.

The question of trade unionism was once more
discussed at our Congress at Eisenach in 1869.
The practice of making admission conditional on

the political faith of the applicant was especially condemned. Greulich spoke in favour of international organisation in order to bring the masses into the unions. The capitalist, he said, is not afraid of our few miserable pence ; it is the masses he fears.

The question of conciliation was again discussed at Stuttgart in 1870, but no solution was achieved. From 1871 onwards, in the years of the great boom, the unions developed rapidly, and began to take rather an independent line. This season of prosperity resulted in numerous strikes, which led to a good deal of trouble on account of the quite insufficient strike funds of the unions. As early as March, 1871, this unsatisfactory state of affairs was discussed by the Social Democratic Society of Leipzig, which published the following resolutions :—

" 1. Strikes are only palliatives, and no permanent remedy.

" 2. The aim of Social-Democracy is not merely to procure higher wages under the present mode of production, but altogether to abolish capitalistic production.

" 3. That with present methods of production wages depend upon supply and demand and cannot be permanently lifted above the standard even by the most successful strikes ;

" 4. That lately several strikes have been contrived by the manufacturers in order to obtain a plausible excuse for raising their prices, and that such strikes do not profit the workers, but only the employers, who raise their prices much more than is justified by the rise in wages.

" 5. That unsuccessful strikes encourage the manufacturers and discourage the workers—a twofold blow to the Labour party ;

" 6. That the large manufacturers have sometimes made an additional profit, the smaller employers finding it impossible to keep their works open, so that the larger firms have been able to sell their stocks at increased prices.

" 7. That it is at present impossible for our party to give financial aid to large bodies of strikers.

" We therefore urge the friends and supporters of our party not to start a strike without urgent necessity and ample means ; and, further, not to proceed heedlessly, but according to a scheme of organisation embracing the whole of Germany. As the best means of providing funds and organisa-- tion the foundation and fostering of trades unions is recommended."

This advice was excellent, but was not followed.

In mid-June, 1872, the first Trade Union Congress met at Frankfort. The matter most discussed was the creation of a centralised executive and of a trade union newspaper. I had developed my programme for the Congress in a newspaper article, in which I said: "The future of the working-classes lies in trade unionism ; it is through trades unions that the masses become class-conscious, learn to fight capitalists, and so naturally become Socialist."

When, after long incarceration in fortress and prison, I was once more at liberty, in the spring of 1875, I was offered the editorship of the Central Trade Union journal, the *Union*, at a salary of £7 10s. per month. I had to refuse, as my business affairs and my political work left me no time to work for trade unionism. But I continued, of course, to give my attention to the movement and to assist it, especially by speaking at meetings. After 1890 it seemed to me that its development was considerably outstripped by that of the Socialist party, principally on account of the insurance laws, which greatly diminished its usefulness. I spoke in this sense at the party Congress in Cologne in 1873. But my pessimism was not justified ; the facts proved me wrong ; the opinion I had from the first formed of trades unionism was magnificently justified, and I was encouraged to renew my efforts to further the movement.

But to return to 1870. The trade union movement was passing through a very difficult time. The Prussian Government, or rather Bismarck, regarded trade unionism, together with the Social-Democratic party, as the deadly enemy of State and society. He found it necessary to take proceedings against them. In Public Prosecutor Tessendorf he found a worthy instrument. The party organisation and a number of trades unions were suppressed. Then came the year 1878, the year of the attempt on the life of the Emperor, and the anti-Socialist laws, which destroyed at one fell blow all that had been built up by years of labour and enormous sacrifices of time, money, energy, and health. But not for ever. Even the strongest power cannot permanently resist the pressure of evolution and the needs of the times. Even Bismarck had to learn this lesson, much to his astonishment.

CHAPTER XI

MY FIRST SENTENCE. THE "INTERNATIONAL." TROUBLE WITH THE LASSALLEANS

The misgovernment of Queen Isabella of Spain, and the favouritism for which she was notorious, had finally driven the parties of the Opposition into open rebellion. When the provisional Government established by those parties found itself unable to agree as to the nature of the government to be permanently adopted, the democracies of several foreign countries thought fit, by resolutions and addresses, to recommend the Spanish people to adopt the republican form of government. Naturally we thought fit to go one better, and to recommend the establishment of a Social-Democratic republic. Now, Spain lacked almost all the conditions necessary to such a venture. Of the 60,000 members who had, according to the newspapers, joined the "International," at least 50,000 had no existence, but were merely the product of a lively fancy. It was a season of exaggeration, greatly to the advantage of the "International." According to the bourgeois journals, the " International " had millions of members scattered over Europe, and funds in proportion. The worthy citizen was terrified at reading in his paper that the treasurer of the " International " had only to open his safe in order to dispatch millions of money to any point where a strike was in progress. I myself was present at a social gathering of the Berlin Press Society when Prince-Smith * told a neighbour in confidence that the General Council of the " International " had just placed a sum of two million francs (£80,000) at the disposal of the coalminers of Belgium. I found it difficult to refrain from laughter, for the General Council would just then have been glad to possess two million centimes. It had great moral influence, but money was always scarce. Even Bismarck was deluded by the exaggerated reports of the power of the " International " at a period shortly after the insurrection of the Commune. He even thought of convoking an International Conference destined to combat the " International," but the English Government would have nothing to do with this delightful plan.

Our " Address to the Spanish People," which Liebknecht had seconded at a public meeting while I as chairman read it and put it to the vote, brought us into conflict with the law. Finally we

* Leader of the Free Trade party in Germany.

were both condemned to three weeks' imprisonment for the propagation of ideas dangerous to the State. We served this term of imprisonment in Leipzig prison, but only towards the end of 1869, as the case was taken to the higher courts.

In addition to the charge of propagating doctrines dangerous to the State we had also to meet an indictment of libelling the Emperor Napoleon. This charge had to be abandoned, as Napoleon had not personally applied to the court as by law demanded, but had made application through his minister at Dresden.

With the year 1868 our quarrel with both wings of the Lassalleans became even more violent. In March, 1869, we convened, in conjunction with the two sections aforesaid, a General Meeting of Saxon workers at Hohenstein. A meeting of our party was called the day before. On my arrival—it was a Sunday morning—I encountered a number of grimy-looking men, who looked as if they had been up all night, running towards the station. I learned that these were Lassalleans (of the Hatzfeldt-Mende wing), who had come, to the number of some eighty to one hundred on the previous evening from Chemnitz, with the avowed intention of breaking up our meeting. Disorder and even violence had ensued, and the mayor of the city had called out the fire-brigade, as the police seemed powerless.

The excitement was intense, and it had been decided to abandon the General Meeting. This, I think, was a blunder, but it could not be helped. I was congratulated upon my absence, as many of the rioters were looking for me—so I was told—uttering threats of violence. Six months later I spoke with striking success at a great demonstration, when some of the men who had taken part in this affair came to me and begged my forgiveness ; they had been set against me, they declared, but greatly regretted their mistake.

For a long time both Liebknecht and I had greatly wished to arrange a personal meeting with von Schweitzer, and a public discussion. So when at a Lassallean meeting at Leipzig the proposal was made to invite Liebknecht and Schweitzer to confront one another in a public meeting in order to discuss their mutual differences and indictments Liebknecht at once accepted, and stated in his *Democratic Weekly* that he would prove that Schweitzer, either for money or from inclination, had systematically obstructed the organisation of the Labour party, thus working in the interests of Bismarckian Cæsarism. Schweitzer at first accepted, then retracted, and finally stated that he would meet us at the General Meeting of the General Union, which was shortly to be held at Barmen-Elberfeld. This meeting I shall refer to in another chapter.

CHAPTER XII

JEAN BAPTIST VON SCHWEITZER AND HIS LEADER-
SHIP OF THE PROLETARIAN LABOUR MOVEMENT.

1. BIOGRAPHICAL

AMONG the notabilities who, after the death of
Lassalle successively took over the leadership of
the General German Labour Union, Jean Baptist
von Schweitzer was by far the most able.

Schweitzer was well endowed with many of the
qualities which are of value to a man in such a
position. He was well grounded in theory, his
political outlook was wide, and his judgment cool.
As a journalist and agitator he had a gift of making
the most difficult problems clear to the most simple
of workmen, and he understood as well as any one
how to fascinate the masses and rouse them to
fanaticism. He published in his paper, the *Sozialdemokrat*, a number of popular articles of a scientific nature which are to this day among the best
things in Socialistic literature—such, for example,
as his criticism of Marx's "Capital." As a par-

liamentarian he was adroit, always quick to seize
an advantage or exploit a situation. Finally, he was
a good speaker, calculating to a nicety how to
impress the masses and his opponents alike.

But beside these fine and even brilliant gifts he
had many defects which made him a dangerous
leader for a Labour party as yet in the first stages
of development. The movement, which he joined
after many failures, was for him only a means to
an end, and this end was his own advancement.
He came into the movement only after and because
he saw no future in his own class and set, being
early in life an outcast therefrom, by his own
fault, so that his last hope of satisfying his ambition
of playing a " star " part such as his gifts demanded
lay in his joining the Labour movement. He
wanted to be, not only its leader but its dictator,
and to exploit it for his own selfish purposes. For
a number of years he had studied under the Jesuits
in one of their institutes ; he had been through
the University, and had read for the law. The
Jesuitical casuistry and legal craftiness thus
obtained, joined to his inborn cunning and
shrewdness, made him a politician capable of
going straight for his purpose without any scruples,
and that purpose was the satisfaction of his ambition at any cost and the indulgence in the life of
a " man about town," for which he lacked the

means. But it is an old story, illustrated by all democratic movements, that leaders who have expensive habits and are sybarites in their lives, yet lack the means to satisfy their tastes, sooner or later become the prey of the tempter, and all the more readily when they seem to obtain a certain amount of apparent success.

The dictatorial power with which the organisation of the General German Labour Union endowed its leader was very favourable to the ends Schweitzer had in view. His domineering position was fortified by the fact that the only paper of the Union—he did not tolerate a second one—was in his hands and edited by him, the *Sozialdemokrat*. Thus the power was in his hands, and he used it without scruple to exercise an absolute intellectual domination over the members of the Union, and forcibly to suppress every contradiction, every expression of opinion inconvenient to him. Yet he had a knack of flattering the masses, whom he really despised, which I have never seen in greater perfection in any man. He spoke of himself as their instrument, bound to do the sovereign will of the people, the "sovereign people" who read nothing but his own paper, and on whom he imposed his will by suggestion. Whosoever dared to kick against the pricks was taxed with the lowest motives, branded as an idiot, or as an "intellectual " who despised the brave, honest workers, and wanted to exploit them in his own interests.

The dominance which Schweitzer gradually attained was only possible while the movement was in its infancy. This must serve as some excuse for his fanatical adherents. Any one attempting to-day to play the part of a Schweitzer would very soon be suppressed, no matter who he might be.

Schweitzer was a democrat in the grand style ; had he been head of a State he would have been a worthy disciple of Macchiavelli, whose principles he adored. The despotic power which he exercised over the Union for so many years can only be compared to certain phenomena in the Roman Catholic Church. He had not in vain sat at the feet of the Jesuits.

What Liebknecht and I accused him of was that he directed the General German Labour Union— of course against the will and without the knowledge of the majority of the members—in the interests of the Bismarckian policy, which we regarded, not as a German but as a Greater Prussian policy, devised in the interests of the Hohenzollern dynasty, which was endeavouring to establish its domination over the whole of Germany, and to imbue it with the Prussian spirit and principles of government—and these are the deadliest enemies of democracy

As matters stood, and considering the great political fight against the Liberal bourgeoisie in which Bismarck was then engaged, he used any and every means, however trivial, which could serve his purpose. In a former chapter I have told of his negotiations with Lassalle. No intelligent and clear-sighted man—and both Lassalle and Schweitzer were such—could have the slightest doubt as to what a Social-Democrat could and could not obtain from Bismarck ; and if Bismarck entered into relations with the Social-Democrats, it was only to exploit them in his own interests, and to throw them away afterwards as one throws away a sucked orange. There was, of course, the explanation that Bismarck bought the Democrat leaders ; but that at least was impossible in the case of Lassalle.

The attempts to exploit the General German Labour Union in the interests of Bismarck's Greater Prussian policy were both prompt and tenacious. I am going to prove that Schweitzer was aware of this plot of Bismarck's and actively worked for it.

Schweitzer was born on the 12th of July, 1834, at Frankfort-on-the-Main. His family was of the so-called Old Patricians of old Frankfort.

He came to Berlin to study law in 1850, and was introduced to leading members of the Prussian

" Reaction," among them to Friedrich Julius Stahl. But his family connections led him to favour the Greater German policy of a united Germany under Austrian hegemony. This he advocated in several pamphlets. Later he became a Republican, and recommended a revolution to bring about the unification of Germany on a democratic basis. After making the acquaintance of Lassalle he went over to Bismarck's policy of a Prussian Germany. While up to the year 1863 he had written and spoken against Prussia and had even said that both Prussia and Austria must be destroyed to make room for a united German Republic, there now came a sudden change. Two very grave scandals had made life in his own class and set impossible. When he met Lassalle at Frankfort in 1863 he promptly recognised that here was an opportunity to assure his future and to satisfy his ambition. In a speech delivered in October, 1863, entitled " The Party of Progress," he violently attacked the Liberal bourgeois parties and maintained that the attacks of the Social-Democratic party ought in the first instance to be directed against the Liberals and not against modern absolutism with its castes of priests and nobles.

According to this theory it was not the supporters of feudalism, to whom every kind of social and political progress was an abomination, who

were the chief enemies of the workers, but the
Liberals, the least radical of whom were yet believers in modern development and advocated a
certain degree of progress, without which the capitalistic order of things could not exist, an order
which holds out to the proletarian at least the
possibility of rising, by his own efforts, to a state
of freedom, and of abolishing the oppression of
man by his fellows. Schweitzer knew that the
doctrine he preached was ultra-reactionary, and
a betrayal of the interests of the workers, but
he advanced it in order to recommend himself to
the ruling powers.

Bismarck the *Junker* of course accepted this
help from the extreme Left (the Radical wing)
with the utmost pleasure, and was even willing to
assist the man who gave it. Was not this playing
with the forces of Socialism and Communism—
and no sane man could take it for more than playing—an excellent way of scaring out of their wits
the Liberal bourgeoisie, who never had a super-
fluity of courage, and of ensnaring it in the meshes
of Bismarckian Cæsarism? The more radical the
Socialism the more it scared the bourgeoisie. I
need hardly emphasise the fact that this policy
is the very antithesis of Democracy and Socialism.

*   *   *   *   *

2. The "Sozialdemokrat."

In July, 1864, Schweitzer came to Berlin to edit a party organ, the *Sozialdemokrat*. The money to start the paper he got from his friend von Hofstetten, who had married a Countess Strachwitz.

The programme which headed the first number —solidarity of democracy all over the world, a unified and powerful Germany on a democratic basis, abolition of the rule of capital, and the predominance in the State of labour—secured him many influential contributors, including Liebknecht, Marx, Engels, Colonel Rüstow, Georg Herwegh, Jean Philip Becker, and Moritz Hess, and would, had he adhered to it, have been of the greatest assistance to the party ; moreover, it would have prevented a split.

But the correct attitude of the *Sozialdemokrat* did not last long. Even in the sixth number there was an article on the Bismarck Cabinet, containing passages which betrayed, if as yet very cautiously, a sympathetic attitude towards Bismarck's policy.

In No. 14 and the following issues appeared the series of articles on "The Bismarck Ministry," in which Schweitzer dropped the democratic mask, and in consequence lost most of the abovementioned contributors. In these articles he attacked parliamentarianism as the rule of mediocrity, extolled Frederic the Great and Prussian and Hohenzollern royalism, and quite correctly stated the then existing condition of the Prussian State to be "unfinished, and calling for further annexations," and in its very essence the adversary of any form of parliamentarianism. In this series he finally reached the conclusion that the only two factors that really counted in Germany were Prussia and the German nation as a whole— " Prussian bayonets and German proletarian fists ! " It seems incredible that he should have found it possible to support such a policy, for did it not mean the complete defeat of Democracy? However, he carefully avoided stating a clear issue ; he left it to the reader to draw his own conclusions. He wanted to capture his readers for Bismarck's policy, by his special pleading for Prussia. In the whole German Press, Bismarck had no abler apologist for his policy.

When Schweitzer's contributors resigned and attacked him in the Press, he pleaded that he had only continued the policy of Lassalle. That may be so ; but Lassalle, who was a wealthy man, could stand up to Bismarck, while Schweitzer, who was deeply in debt, became simply one of Bismarck's tools.*

* Herr Bebel describes the curious double dealing of Schweitzer at great length, with documentary evidence.

The policy of the *Sozialdemokrat* quickly brought forth the desired fruits. As early as February, 1865, a member of the General German Labour Union made a speech in which he stated his preference for the existing Prussian Reactionary Ministry over a Ministry of Progressive Liberals. A Congress of the Workmen of Rhenish Westphalia adopted a resolution recommending the policy of the *Sozialdemokrat* and approving its attitude toward the Prussian Government, which had promised measures to improve the condition of the working-classes, and might even introduce universal suffrage. This resolution was nothing less than a vote of confidence in Bismarck and the Prussian Government.

The opposition which soon found voice against the dictatorial attitude of Schweitzer was condemned as sacrilegious to the memory of Lassalle. This worship of Lassalle, which, of course, suited Schweitzer's plans, gradually became almost idiotic, and developed into a sort of religious orthodoxy. The subject of " Christ and Lassalle " was for years the stock subject of discussion in public meetings. F. W. Fritsche, who spoke on this subject in Berlin in the year 1868, was even tried for blasphemy, but was acquitted, criminal intent not being proven.

When Schweitzer found he had shown his hand too openly he would write as a Radical. He could also write as a Reactionary, as when he published a long report on the celebration of the King's birthday, by the members of the General German Labour Union, who even sent the King a telegram of congratulation as the " friend of the workers."

The circulation of the *Sozialdemokrat* was at this time very small : there were only a few hundred subscribers. The paper accordingly needed a considerable subvention, and could pay no salary to its two editors, who were yet dependent on it. Yet in spite of its miserable financial outlook, it became a daily paper from the 1st of July, 1865. This nearly doubled its deficit, without apparently promising an increased circulation. The question was natural : Who provides the money? The General Union did not require or profit by the enlargement of the paper ; but the Conservative Press reprinted, with the utmost delight, the *Sozialdemokrat's* violent attacks upon the Liberal party and its policy, which forced the Liberal Press to pay an amount of attention to the *Sozialdemokrat* which was out of all proportion to its real influence. One Liberal paper openly accused the *Sozialdemokrat* of keeping in close touch with Bismarck, in order to obtain the necessary funds from ultra-Conservative sources. When requested by Schweitzer to retract, it absolutely declined to do so, and defied Schweitzer to go to law. Schweitzer threatened to do so, but of course did not dare.

In those days one Preuss, a man claiming to be a worker, made himself notorious. He was suspected of being in the service of the Government, and more especially in that of Privy-Councillor Wagener, who was Bismarck's right hand in all social and political matters. This man Preuss was a frequent speaker at the meetings of the General German Labour Union. The chain was thus complete—Preuss, Schweitzer, Wagener, Bismarck. Schweitzer never met Bismarck personally. He was no Lassalle. I shall never forget how one day when Schweitzer mounted the tribune of the Diet to make a speech, Bismarck, with assumed curiosity, held up his eye-glasses and examined him from top to toe, as much as to say : " So this is the man that hangs to my coat-tails ! "

The Berlin police probably knew of his relations with the Government, for the *Doktor*, as he was familiarly called, was always most cordially received by them.

Countess Hatzfeldt, the intimate friend of Lassalle, in whose opinion Schweitzer by no means went far enough in his advocacy of Bismarck's policy, thought to justify his support of it in a letter written in 1864 to the wife of Herwegh :—

" There is a world of difference between these

two things : to sell oneself to an opponent, and to work for him secretly or openly, or, as a great politician to grasp the opportunity, to profit by the mistakes of an opponent, to make your enemies destroy one another, to drive your adversary on to slippery ground. . . . Mere honest minds, such as regard things always from an ideal standpoint of a future State, a standpoint suspended in mid-air, may be very good people in their own way, and privately, but they are of no account in action, they cannot direct the course of events ; they are good enough in the mass to follow their leader, who knows better."

The gracious Countess here developed a programme which would have shipwrecked a Lassalle, because he had not behind him the driving power to carry such a policy through. It is my firm conviction that if Lassalle had joined issue with Bismarck he would have been beaten ; an attempt to play Bismarck at his own game must have ended in a pitiable fiasco. To believe that a Bismarck could or would make real concessions to Social-Democracy, the deadliest enemy of bourgeois society, while it was of the utmost importance that he should seek an understanding with the modern forces of capitalism, to which end he might even exploit Social-Democracy—to believe such a thing would be a proof of blindness disastrous to one engaged in " Realpolitik." Social-Democracy is not a flock of sheep to follow its bell-wether blindly or a pig to be led by the nose. Countess Hatzfeldt may have thought as much at the time, under the influence of her surroundings, but to-day a democratic policy is impossible without the conscious co-operation of the masses and an adherence to honest and open tactics. The masses will not put up with any diplomatic finessing ; a leader who should think otherwise would soon learn his lesson.

When opportunity offered Schweitzer again turned ultra-Radical. This was his usual method of disarming criticism and silencing his opponents in the union. For some days his *Sozialdemokrat* was confiscated. Finally he was condemned, on a charge of *lèse-majesté* and other offences, to sixteen months' imprisonment. But this sentence did not interrupt his journalistic work. He edited his paper from prison ; his correspondence was not restricted ; he received numerous visitors. It had been said that his former terms of imprisonment were proof that he was no agent of Bismarck. This is not the case ; a Government does not reveal its relations with its political agents to the Courts. A temporary imprisonment of a political agent is even a very useful means of disarming suspicion. Thus at a time when Lassalle was having long and frequent political conversations with Bismarck as "an agreeable country neighbour," he was, nevertheless, condemned by the Berlin courts to a number of sharp terms of imprisonment. In the months which preceded the war of 1866 the *Sozialdemokrat* worked consistently in the interests of Bismarck's policy. Quite forgetting his former confession of faith, Schweitzer openly preached the overthrow of Austria. "Austria," he said, "should be reduced to the thirteen millions of inhabitants who belonged to the German Confederation. Only thus could a United Germany be constituted, when Prussia would be in possession of the field."

On the 9th of May, 1866, he was released from prison on account of his bad health. Yet immediately after his release he took a most active part in politics, proving not only that the "state of health" was a pretext, but also that the Government was not averse to his activities ; for, as a rule, if a political prisoner is released, it is on condition that he does not continue the course of action which led to his imprisonment.

After what has been said it is hardly necessary to contradict the contention, lately renewed, that Schweitzer and his Union exerted any real influence on the course of events—that is, in the matter of obtaining universal suffrage. Of course Bismarck accepted help for his reforms where he could find it. As early as 1863, when the General Union had just been formed, he had, as a counter-move against the Austrian Reform proposal, demanded a German Parliament elected by universal suffrage. Thus he wrote, in 1866, in a circular dispatch :—

" Direct elections and universal suffrage I hold to be a greater safeguard for a conservative attitude (of the masses) than some " fancy franchise " designed to produce preconceived majorities. According to our experience, the masses are more honestly interested in the preservation of good order than the leaders of those classes to which some kind of property qualification would give a privileged status."

And in the same year he wrote to Count Bernsdorff, then Prussian Ambassador to the Court of St. James :—

" I may state the conviction, based on long experience, that the artificial system of indirect elections and by classes of electors is much more dangerous, because it prevents the supreme power from getting into touch with the healthy elements which constitute the heart of the populace. . . . The makers of revolutions are the electoral colleges, which provide the revolutionary party with a net stretching all over the country, which is easy of manipulation, as was seen in the case of the " electors " of Paris in 1799. I do not hesitate to declare that indirect elections are a most important aid to revolution, and I think I have gathered a good deal of practical experience in these matters."

This clearly reflects the annoyance which the Prussian three-class electoral system caused him. This system had twice returned a formidable majority against the Government. Again, in the conglomeration of States which constituted the North German Confederation, no other electoral basis than universal suffrage was possible. The Radical Labour Societies of Leipzig had demanded it as early as 1862, and since 1865 it had been on the programme of all Labour organisations.

Schweitzer once went so far as to defend Bismarck, when the latter, fearing that the delegates would again refuse money to carry on the war (1866), adjourned the Prussian Diet.

On the 1st of April, 1866, the *Sozialdemokrat* ceased publication as a daily paper and returned to its three issues a week. It had then 500 regular subscribers. When, after the war, Austria ceded Venetia to France, Schweitzer took the opportunity of deserting to the Prussian camp, " the astonishing organising power of Prussia having proved that Germany could look for salvation only from that quarter."

But when the draft of the Constitution of the North German Confederation was at last published,

even Schweitzer, in a fit of belated pessimism, confessed in his paper that the German people had not
looked for a German unity of that particular type.
Bismarck, the thorough-going "Realpolitiker," had
struck the iron while it was hot, creating a Constitution which was decidedly less liberal even than that
of Prussia. Schweitzer, who was so well aware
of the character of the Prussian State and of
Bismarck, ought to have foreseen the event. We,
who cherished no illusions, were not disappointed.

3. Schweitzer as a Parliamentarian and as a Dictator of the General Labour Union.

At the time of the elections to the Constituent
North German Diet, in February, 1867, Schweitzer
made it abundantly clear in his *Sozialdemokrat*
that the Conservatives would not find him inclined
to be disobliging. He evidently counted on making
a bargain with them against the Liberals, whom
he once more attacked with the utmost violence.
He was a candidate in the constituency of Barmen-
Elberfeld ; his opponents were Bismarck and a
Liberal. But he did not survive the first ballot ; so
the second ballot lay between Bismarck and the
Liberal. In one of his Macchiavellian speeches
he counselled his supporters to "follow the call
of the heart," and almost all the Social-Democratic
votes went to Bismarck, who was duly elected.

Schweitzer sought to justify his advice by declaring that he had intended to give the Liberal bourgeoisie a lesson. The votes given to Bismarck by the workers were given to him, not as a Conservative candidate, but rather as the Minister who had of his own accord granted the people a right—the right of universal suffrage—which the Liberal Opposition had persistently neglected to demand. Schweitzer also opposed my election at Glauchau-Meerane, because, to a pure Lassallean, I was " a traitor to the cause." When a second election became necessary at Elberfeld through the withdrawal of Bismarck, who had been elected to a second constituency, Schweitzer was again a candidate, and went to the second ballot against the Liberal, who was the well-known Professor von Gneist. But he was again rejected, although he openly claimed the votes of the Conservatives as a *quid pro quo* for his services to Bismarck in the previous election, stating that the Labour party and the Conservatives could very well work together in the cause of social reform.

At last Schweitzer was duly elected, in August, 1867, by the help of Conservative votes, and made his entrance into the first North German Reichstag. The leader of the Conservative party had even paid some £60 towards his election expenses. Schweitzer was duly grateful, and promised that although he would always vote with the extreme Left in matters touching the freedom and welfare of the people, he would always, with all his might, support the King of Prussia and his Government in all questions of foreign policy or when danger threatened the Fatherland, and this inside and outside the Reichstag.

Schweitzer's election very naturally evoked great enthusiasm among his supporters, which he exploited by driving a four-in-hand with a team of white horses in triumphal progress through the two cities of Barmen and Elberfeld. Schweitzer delighted in such triumphal progresses, the like of which would certainly terminate the career of any Labour leader who should indulge in them to-day. He repeated them on various occasions; for example, the four-in-hand with the white team was prominent during the whole time of the meeting of the General Union at Cassel. But when he presented the bill—by no means a moderate one —the meeting agreed to pay the cost of his progress from the station to the town, but no more!

In the debates in the North German Reichstag, Liebknecht and I had not a few personal encounters with Schweitzer, he surreptitiously defending the policy of Bismarck, while attacking us as standing outside the Fatherland in its new form.

In May, 1867, Schweitzer had at last reached the

goal of his ambition, and was elected President of the General Union. The Union was in a bad way, especially in respect of its finances. Against his election it was argued that he was generally distrusted, and that the combination of the presidency and the editorship of the organ of the Union in one person was unsatisfactory. After being elected he solemnly shook hands with each delegate and promised to do everything in his power to advance the cause of the General Union, while the delegates promised with equal solemnity to stand by the Union and its president. Thus a kind of "Oath of the Tennis Court" was taken, like that of the National Assembly of France in 1789, with the difference that in this case the chief actor in the scene knew that he was playing a comedy.

His *Sozialdemokrat* at this time had a circulation of some 1,200 copies, and as he had recently broken with his friend von Hofstetten, in a manner not much to his own credit, Hofstetten having lost all his money in the venture, the question was once more heard, where did he get the money for his paper and his rather luxurious way of living? We knew from information gathered in Berlin that he led a dissolute life. During the sessions of the Reichstag he kept a coach with liveried servants, and gave champagne dinners to his intimates. As he had on a previous occasion embezzled money from the funds of a rifle club, so he now, as President of the General Union, embezzled money from the funds composed of the pence of ill-paid working-men in order to satisfy his appetites. The sums were small, but that was not Schweitzer's fault ; the Union was far from wealthy. Schweitzer was more than once publicly accused of this shameful action, but he never dared to defend himself. A man capable of such mean conduct is certainly capable of selling his political services, the only tolerably profitable business open to him. It is impossible to prove such things ; one can only judge by circumstantial evidence. Bismarck at this time had the handling of the interest of a capital sum of some £2,400,000, the private property of the King of Hanover, which had been sequestrated in 1866. The manner in which Bismarck employed this money for political purposes gained it the title of the " Reptile Fund." It is a characteristic fact that while the whole Opposition Press denounced this political corruption, Schweitzer never so much as mentioned it in the *Sozial-demokrat*.

It is no less characteristic of Schweitzer that he never in his paper mentioned our journal, the *Democratic Weekly*, by name, but always spoke of it as " Herr Liebknecht's paper." He did this lest any of his readers should conceive the idea of taking in the *Democratic Weekly*. This was a petty and ridiculous method of fighting us.

At the next General Meeting of the Union, Schweitzer made an announcement which was in a way a denunciation of himself. " This will be our last General Meeting," he said. " The hostility of the Prussian Government will declare itself. The Union will be dissolved." And, in fact, the Union was dissolved, three weeks later, by the Leipzig police, the Union being then domiciled in that city. Can there be any doubt that the dissolution of the Union was agreed upon by Schweitzer in concert with the Berlin police? Naturally Schweitzer made no protest, and the Union ceased to be. Now, if it had been by the hostility of the Prussian Government that the Union was destroyed, would it not have been Schweitzer's duty to withdraw it as far as possible from the hostile influence of that Government, and to select as its domicile some city outside Prussia—such as Hamburg, for instance? For in Hamburg no law against association was in existence. No ; instead of this he chose Berlin, thereby proving conclusively his relations with the Berlin police.

The new Union was formed in " secret conclave," and the new statutes gave the President almost despotic power. Meanwhile, Schweitzer had once more to serve a three-months term of imprisonment, but was liberated after less than a month, "on account of family matters." But he was at once deeply engaged in political work, and although the term of his sentence would not be at an end by then, he fixed the date of the next General Meeting of the Union for the 27th of March, the place to be Barmen-Elberfeld. But he knew beforehand that the authorities would release him.

His attitude towards us became more violent than ever. He accused us of working, consciously or otherwise, for the Austrian policy. I will admit that Liebknecht, in his *Democratic Weekly*, had lately adopted an attitude towards Austria which I had protested against, and Schweitzer, of course, exploited this weakness of Liebnecht's to the utmost.

Six weeks before the meeting at Barmen-Elberfeld, Schweitzer was duly elected President by 5,000 votes against 54. But it was a moral defeat : the Union had then some 12,000 members, so that the majority had not voted at all.

In the Reichstag I was the involuntary witness of a meeting between Schweitzer and Prince Albrecht, brother of the King, who was a member. When the Prince saw Schweitzer approaching him, he beckoned to him, shook him vigorously by the hand, and said in a most amiable tone :—

"How do you do, my dear Schweitzer ! "

Schweitzer : " Thank you, your Royal Highness."

The Prince: " And why have you not been present at the sitting? "

Schweitzer : " I was there, your Royal Highness."

Prince : " Why did you not speak? You were expected to do so. . . ."

I went off, not wishing to be caught eavesdropping. But the few words I heard conclusively proved that Schweitzer was well known to the Prince, and that those on the right side of the House knew exactly what even his most Radical speeches really meant.

4. THE CONGRESS AT BARMEN-ELBERFELD. REVOLT AGAINST SCHWEITZER WITHIN THE GENERAL LABOUR UNION.

When we arrived at Barmen-Elberfeld on the 27th of March we were welcomed by a number of friendly members of the " International."

Schweitzer had previously announced in the *Sozialdemokrat* that the enemy had on two occasions dared to raise its head against the president (who was also the most prominent and important person in the Union), and that the General Meeting was expected to repel all attacks upon the organisation.

At the preliminary meeting it was decided, contrary to the advice of Schweitzer, to admit us at

once. On the following afternoon Liebknecht and
I entered the crowded hall under the fire of the
furious glances of Schweitzer's fanatical adherents.
Liebknecht spoke first for an hour and a half ; I
followed with a much shorter speech. Our speeches
contained a summary of all the accusations we
had levelled against Schweitzer. There were
several violent interruptions, especially when we
accused him of being a Government agent ; but
I refused to withdraw anything. The *Sozialdemokrat* published a very greatly condensed and confusing report of our speeches. Liebknecht, from
motives of exaggerated loyalty, restricted himself
to a mere statement of facts in his *Democratic
Weekly*, adding that he would publish no more
attacks upon Schweitzer, as there was still some
hope of coming to an understanding with the
other wing.

Schweitzer, who sat behind us when we spoke,
did not utter a word in reply. We left at once,
some of the delegates guarding us against assault
from the fanatical supporters of Schweitzer, amid
a storm of imprecations, such as " Knaves ! "
" Traitors ! " " Rascals ! " and so forth. At the
doors our friends met us and took us under their
protection, escorting us in safety to our hotel.

Schweitzer obtained a vote of confidence from
the delegates by a majority of 6,500 votes,

delegates representing 4,500 votes abstaining from the vote. But he had to pay dearly for his victory. The organisation of the Union, which, after its dissolution by the Leipzig police, had been imposed upon it by Schweitzer, and which gave him dictatorial power, was now remodelled, the meeting adopting a thoroughly democratic organisation in its place, which greatly restricted the power of the president.

Deprived of the absolute power, Schweitzer tried to come to an understanding with us in Berlin. He invited us to dinner, and even took us to the play in his carriage and pair. We negotiated a truce, agreeing not to attack one another's organisations, and to co-operate in the Reichstag. Identical declarations to this effect were published in our respective papers.

All seemed for the best ; but Schweitzer chafed under the democratic constitution of the Union which had been voted at Barmen-Elberfeld, and the restrictions under which it placed him. It was political extinction for him, as it effectively prevented any further double-dealing. He made up his mind to escape from the situation. Like a bolt from the blue the *Sozialdemokrat* published a proclamation, under the title " Restoration of Unity in the Lassallean Party." In bombastic terms it proclaimed the restoration of the old Lassallean organisation and the re-combination of the two wings, Schweitzer's contingent and that founded by the Countess Hatzfeldt, the intimate friend of Lassalle. With the utmost precipitation the two separate Unions were dissolved, and Lassalle's organisation reinstituted. This *coup d'état* was designed to restore Schweitzer's old predominance. At the same time it was declared that the truce with our organisation was at an end, as we had been the first to break it. I was supposed to be the culprit; and my offence consisted in the fact that I had poached upon the preserves of the General Union by speaking at meetings presided over by members of that Union, claiming that Social-Democratic principles were the sole means of improving the conditions of the workers, and that the several branches of the Labour party should work together in alliance.

I may add that although I gained success and applause as a propagandist I wrote to my wife about this time that I was sick of the work. Yet how long I had to continue it! But it was my duty, and that was enough.

The *coup d'état* on the part of Schweitzer greatly incensed a considerable section of the General Union. Some of the more intelligent members recognised that Schweitzer was impossible, and that he was the main obstacle to unity. A member from

Hamburg, Bracke, asked Liebknecht and myself to appoint a meeting. We met, with other members, at a third-rate hotel at Magdeburg. Some were in favour of immediate action, others of reform from within We replied that the meeting at Barmen-Elberfeld had proved that that was impossible so long as Schweitzer was president. We talked all night, and finally Bracke, bent over the billiard-table, wrote a proclamation. We went to bed at 3 a.m. The proclamation, addressed to all friends of the party, stigmatised Schweitzer's action as hypocritical and insulting to the sovereign people, and as tending, not to unite all Social-Democratic workers in one party, but to increase the gulf between the different sections. It asked all workers to rise in revolt against the rule of a single man, and promised at once to call a Congress of all the Social-Democratic workers of Germany, in order to found a Social-Democratic party on a democratic basis, in conjunction with the " International." The proclamation was signed by twelve members of the General Union, who made a declaration of their secession at the time, and was published on the 26th of June in the *Democratic Weekly*. As we laid particular stress upon our honesty of purpose, against the dishonest methods of Schweitzer, we soon earned the nickname of " the honest men."

The standing committee of our Association resolved unanimously (on a motion of mine) to accede
to the proclamation and to circularise our societies,
urging them to do the same, and to call for a
General German Social-Democratic Labour Congress. I also wrote to the German section of the
Central Council of the "International" at Geneva,
asking them to approve of our work of unification.

Schweitzer, of course, opposed us by his usual
methods in the *Sozialdemokrat*. He maintained
that ours was not a party of working-men, but
of literary men, schoolmasters, and other "bourgeois." He also claimed that Lassalle's organisation, which had been restored, must be kept intact.
We, on the other hand, published in the *Democratic
Weekly* daily lists of secessions from the Union,
which included many trades-union leaders.

Schweitzer was re-elected president with an
absolute majority; but the figures were not published. He stated that the General Union would
send delegates to the Social-Democratic Congress
and published a number of resolutions to be moved.
At the same time he maintained that behind our
Congress stood the whole of the Liberal bourgeoisie
of every shade. We replied by asking him not to
send his tools, but to come himself. But he preferred to go to prison once more.

I will offer the following facts to the reader's

consideration : At the end of November, 1869, Schweitzer went to prison for three months.   At the end of December he was released—for a week —in order to settle certain family affairs consequent upon the death of his father.   He was free for seven weeks, which he spent in the most intense political activity, under the very eyes of the police, until he returned to prison on the 18th of February. On the 4th of March he was again released for the Session of the Reichstag.   The Session ended on June 22nd ; but Schweitzer was free until the 19th of July, and was actively agitating all the time.   He returned to prison only when he found it convenient.

Now, in no other case were the Prussian police so considerate.   On the contrary, it was their brutal custom to pull those sentenced to imprisonment out of their beds at six in the morning.   Schweitzer never saw this side of the police.   Was not our distrust of him justified?

Just before the Congress of Eisenach one of the Lassalleans sought to damage my political reputation.   He maintained, in the *Sozialdemokrat*, that I received an annual pension of 600 thalers (about £90) from the ex-King of Hanover.   The accusation was a silly one, yet members of the General Union believed it.   I therefore decided to go to law and to prosecute my accuser for malicious libel.   I con-

sulted one Hirsemenzel, then the first advocate in
Berlin. But he declined to take up my case ; the
court, he said, would not find that there was anything derogatory in the contention that I was in
the pay of a prince, and would find my traducer
guilty of libel merely. This would not satisfy me.
Further, if the Minister of the Household of the
ex-King were called as a witness he would certainly
refuse to attend, which would tell against me. In
the end I wrote to my accuser, challenging him
to publish his proofs. Instead of withdrawing his
accusation he repeated it, and defied me to bring
an action against him. I then called him a low
slanderer, and challenged him to bring an action
against me in the Leipzig courts, as I had no faith
in the Berlin courts. In the end it all came to
nothing, my accuser asserting that he himself had
no proofs, but that a high Government official had
declared that the accusation was true ; he, however,
would give proof of it only in court.

5. THE CONGRESS OF EISENACH. THE FOUNDATION
OF THE SOCIAL-DEMOCRATIC LABOUR PARTY AND
THE DISSOLUTION OF THE LEAGUE OF WORKING-
MEN'S SOCIETIES.

After it had been agreed among us that the
Congress should be convened at Eisenach, on the
7th of August, a manifesto was published in the

Democratic Weekly on the 17th of July, signed by 66 ex-members of the General Union, 114 members of the Association of German Working-men's Societies, some members of the Lassallean (Hatzfeldt) Union, the Central Committee of German Labour Unions in Switzerland, the German Republican Society of Zurich, some Austrian Labour representatives, and by J. P. Becker for the German branch of the " International."

The manifesto was addressed to the German Social-Democrats. After recalling the internal dissension in the Labour party caused by the necessity of opposing the selfish and malignant tactics of certain individuals, and expressing the hope that the party would emerge from this healthful revolution with increased purity of principles and unity of organisation, on the same basis as the " International," it called for a General German Social-Democratic Labour Congress, to be held at Eisenach, from the 7th to the 9th of August. The agenda included : (1) Organisation of the party. (2) Programme of the party. (3) The relation of the party to the " International." (4) The party organ. (5) Federation of trades unions. The delegates were asked to arrive without fail on the 7th, in order to elect a committee and agree as to the order of business.

At the same time I called a Congress of the

German Working-men's Societies for the 9th of August, also to be held at Eisenach, to discuss the attitude of our Association towards the new organisation of the Social-Democratic party, and eventually its own dissolution. The conveners of the Eisenach Congress also gave me the mandate to make all necessary arrangements at Eisenach, and to elaborate a draft programme and plan of organisation for general discussion.

It is not without a certain glee that I turn over the old letters in which the Royal Saxon Railway and the then private Thuringian Railway granted my request that they would allow the members of the Social-Democratic Congress the reduced fares generally granted to Congress visitors. We should not be so lucky as to get such terms to-day !

At the outset J. Ph. Becker caused me some embarrassment by an article which he contributed to his *Vorboten* (Forerunner) dealing with the organisation of the new party. Now, Jean Philippe was a splendid old fellow, devoted to the cause, ready for any sacrifice, indefatigable day and night, an old stager who in the revolution in Baden in 1848 was a colonel of Irregulars, and would have liked nothing so well as once more to have found himself in the saddle. He used to tell any amount of amusing stories of his full and rather stormy life ; I have listened to him for hours at a time. But

he did not know very much about party organisation, and his long absence from Germany had left
him a stranger to contemporary German conditions.
Instead of a compact, centralised, yet democratic-
ally organised party capable of energetic action,
Becker proposed a loosely knit association which
was to propagate democratic principles, but was
to have no party organisation ; it was to be
governed by an organisation of a changeable
character, capable of all developments and dependent upon Geneva. As a result of this article
the General Council of the " International " wrote
to me from London that they knew nothing of it
and did not approve of it. I replied that I was
glad to hear as much, as I should have to oppose
it in the Congress as impracticable.

The Congress was exceedingly well attended.
There were 262 delegates, representing 193 different
localities, among others Becker (Geneva), Greulich
and Dr. Ladendorf (Zurich), Oberwinder and Schoen
(Vienna), and Hofstetten (Berlin). Sonnemann
(Frankfort) was also present, but this was the
last Labour Congress he attended ; his hope
that the Labour party and the People's (Radical)
party would come to an understanding was
never fulfilled. The class characteristics of our
party were repellent to him. The Schweitzerians,
as we thenceforth called the members of the

General Union, were much less numerous, not exceeding half our numbers. They foregathered in the "Ship," we in the "Golden Bear." As we had learned from several quarters that the Schweitzerians intended to break up the Congress by violent means, I went to the Burgomaster and the police, and asked them what they would do in such a case. They assured me that we could do as we liked; there were no restrictions as to the right of association and meeting in Saxe-Weimar; but if the other parties attempted to disturb our arrangements by a display of violence, the police were ready to intervene on our behalf.

About seven in the evening the Schweitzerians, over a hundred strong, marched into the "Golden Bear." When they came to the staircase, which was strongly occupied by our men, they preferred to obtain peaceful admittance by showing their cards. We had arranged beforehand that should any disturbance occur the chairman was to adjourn the Congress until the following day, a Sunday, when the Schweitzerians would be excluded.

It was as we had expected: violent altercations commenced at the very outset at the election of the officers of the Congress. As the lighting was miserable, we at the committee table had stuck a number of candles into bottles, which we had to hold on to with both hands to prevent their toppling over. Finally the assembly became so uproarious that the chairman adjourned it, announcing that it would be resumed on the following morning at 10 a.m. in the "Moor," when only members with yellow cards would be admitted.

Our coup succeeded. All night we sorted out the cards belonging to the Schweitzerians and sent them back. Thenceforth the Congress proceeded with its business without further disturbance.

The draft programme and plan of organisation proposed by the conveners of the Congress were voted with very slight modification. The new party was named the Social-Democratic Labour party. The programme adopted was as follows :—

" 1. The Social-Democratic Labour party aims at the establishment of a free Democratic State (*freier Volksstaat*).

" 2. Every member of the party pledges himself to insist with all his might on the following principles :—

" (*a*) The present political and social conditions are in the highest degree unjust and therefore to be opposed with the utmost energy.

" (*b*) The struggle for the emancipation of the working-classes is not a struggle for class privileges and prerogatives, but for equal rights and equal duties and for the abolition of all class domination.

" (c) The economic dependence of the worker on the capitalist is the basis of his servitude in all its forms, and the Social-Democratic party aims, by the abolition of the present method of production (the wages system) at assuring, by means of co-operative labour, that every worker shall receive the full product of his work.

" (d) Political freedom is the indispensable basis of the economic emancipation of the working-classes. The social question is therefore inseparable from the political question ; its solution depends upon the solution of the political question and is only possible in a democratic State.

" (e) In consideration of the fact that the political and economic emancipation of the working-class is only possible if this class wages war in common and united, the Social-Democratic Labour party adopts a united organisation which yet makes it possible for every one of its members to make his influence felt for the benefit of the whole.

" (f) Considering that the emancipation of labour is neither a local nor a national but a social question, which embraces all countries in which there is a modern society, the Social-Democratic Labour party regards itself, as far as the laws of association permit, as a branch of the "International," and adopts its aims.

3. The following are to be regarded as the most urgent questions of propaganda :—

" (a) Equal universal and direct suffrage by secret ballot for all men over twenty, in the elections for the Reichstag, the Diets of the several Federal States, the provincial and local assemblies, and all other representative bodies. The deputies are to be paid salaries.

" (b) The introduction of direct legislation (Initiative and Referendum) by the people.

" (c) Abolition of all privileges of class, property, birth, and creed.

" (d) Substitution of a National Militia for standing armies.

" (e) Separation of Church and State and secularisation of schools.

" (f) Compulsory education in Elementary Schools and gratuitous instruction in all public educational establishments.

" (g) Independence of the Courts, introduction of the jury system, industrial courts, public and oral procedure, and gratuitous jurisdiction.

" (h) Abolition of all legal restriction of the Press, the right of association and combination, the introduction of a normal working day, the restriction of female labour, and the abolition of child labour.

" (i) Abolition of all indirect taxation and the

introduction of a single direct progressive income tax and a tax on inheritance.

" (j) State help for co-operative undertakings and State credit for free productive co-operative associations, with democratic guarantees." *

In the course of the transactions I was able to announce that Dr. Ladendorf had promised us, from the Revolutionary Fund (Zurich), a sum of 900 thalers (some £45) for purposes of propaganda. This was the source of our means, and not a grant from the King of Hanover. The party organ, the *Volksstaat,* was to be published twice a week.

Wolfenbüttel, in Brunswick, was to be the

---

* The rest of the Eisenach programme lays down the rules for the organisation of the party. The membership fee was fixed at one penny per month, which was not required from those who were regular subscribers of the party organ. A General Congress was to be held annually; the Executive to be elected annually, and to consist of a chairman, vice-chairman, secretary, treasurer (to deposit guarantees), and an assistant. A committee of eleven was to be elected as a committee of control, its duties being : to supervise the financial conduct of the executive, and to hear complaints against the same. It had the power to suspend members of the Executive or the Executive as a body. The *Democratic Weekly* was to be the party organ, and was to be known as the *Volksstaat* ; it was to be under the control of the Executive, with power of appeal to the Committee of Control, and finally to the Party Congress.

headquarters of the executive committee, and Vienna that of the committee of control. I protested against the choice of Leipzig, as we in Leipzig were sure to rub along smoothly enough with the executive, while the Brunswick members had mostly belonged to the General Union and required looking after. Stuttgart was selected for the next Congress. Liebknecht would represent us at the next meeting of the "International" at Basle.

The splendid success of our Congress greatly depressed the Schweitzerians. As they had been excluded, they voted a number of resolutions at their own meeting, but nothing came of that.

At the meeting of our Association, which followed directly upon the Congress, the dissolution of the Association and its incorporation with the Social-Democratic party was unanimously voted. After six years' existence the Association had 119 branches (associated societies) and a membership of 10,000. The books, letters, proclamations, &c., were entrusted to my safe keeping.

6. AFTER EISENACH. THE END OF SCHWEITZER

After the Congress of Eisenach the fight between the two Social-Democratic factions was waged more fiercely than ever before. Even the two Lassallean sections, that led by Schweitzer and the Mende-Hatzfeldt section, were again at loggerheads. Within our own ranks we had some difficulty on account of a resolution touching the land question which had been adopted by the International Labour Congress at Basle. Liebknecht was one of our delegates at this Congress, and the two resolutions which he supported were, firstly, "that society has the right to abolish private property in land and to nationalise the soil," and secondly, "that it is necessary to nationalise the soil." These resolutions caused great excitement in Germany, especially in the ranks of the Progressive Democratic party, which condemned them as an enormity. Liebknecht tried to smooth matters over by declaring, in his *Democratic Weekly*, that it was not a party principle, and that every member of the party could hold his own opinion on the matter. This, of course, did not improve the state of affairs, and gave a handle to the Lassalleans, who branded us as half-baked Socialists and political log-rollers. And when later on Liebknecht radically changed his opinion, and stated in his paper—which since the Eisenach Congress had become the *Volksstaat*— that the Basle resolutions were party principles, he may have been correct, but he was absolutely repudiating his former opinion. I had occasion to defend the Basle resolutions during a journey which I made through the south of Germany for purposes of agitation. In twenty days I spoke at eighteen public meetings in as many towns. At Stuttgart the whole staff of the Progressive (Radical) Democratic party was among the audience, and their leader asked me how our party stood with regard to the Basle resolutions. I replied that our next Congress would define its position, and would doubtless accept them, but I added, to console him, that he need not take it too hardly, as the execution of the resolutions would not be possible until public opinion had been converted. This was gilding the pill.

In the beginning of 1870 a fourth Social-Democratic organisation came into being, but had only a short life. Already there was our organisation and the two Lassallean parties. Schweitzer had used every means at his command to suppress a separate Bavarian organisation, whose organ was the *Proletarian,* published at Augsburg. When this party convened a Congress at Augsburg for the purpose of founding a separate organisation I was sent as a delegate to dissuade them from their purpose, to dispel their suspicions—for they took us for an annexe of the Progressive party—and to persuade them to join our own organisation. Although I did my best I did not then succeed ; but at the following Stuttgart Congress an understanding was arrived at, and the Bavarian section then joined our party. At a meeting which I subsequently addressed at Munich, Georg von Vollmar, then a young man of twenty, was among the audience, as he told me later on.

The second Congress of the Social-Democratic Labour party was held at Stuttgart, on the 4th to 7th of June, 1870. In accordance with the constitution of the North German Confederation the general elections to the Reichstag—which, as it happened, were postponed by the outbreak of the Franco-German War—were to be held by the end of August. The tactics to be observed at the elections were, therefore, the chief subject of discussion at the Congress. Liebknecht and I, who held different opinions as to the scope of practical parliamentary activity, had finally agreed on the following resolution :—

" The Social-Democratic Labour party shall participate in the elections from the purely tactical standpoint of agitation. The representatives of the party in the Reichstag shall act, as far as possible, in the interests of the working-classes, but shall, on the whole, assume a purely negative attitude and use every occasion to prove that the debates are absolutely futile and farcical.

" The party shall not enter into any alliance or compromise with any other party, but the Congress recommends that in constituencies where the party has no candidate of its own, members should give their votes to those who most nearly approach our political standpoint, especially if the candidates are genuine Labour candidates."

Although our resolution was opposed in favour of complete abstention, it was finally adopted.

As to the Basle resolutions, I, as the reporter, proposed the following resolution :—

"Considering that the necessities of production as well as the laws of agronomy (scientific agriculture) demand working on a large scale, and, as in modern industry, the introduction of machinery, and the organisation of rural labour, it is evident that on the whole the modern economic development of agriculture tends in the direction of large holdings ; considering that in agriculture the small and moderately large owners are being gradually supplanted by the owners of large estates, and that the misery and servitude of the majority of the rural population continually increases to the profit of a small minority, which is against all humanity and justice ; considering that the productive potentialities of the soil, which do not depend upon the application of labour, form the raw material of all products and all useful things.

"The Congress gives it as its opinion that the economic development of modern society renders the transformation of all agricultural property into collective property a social necessity, and that the State should grant leases to co-operative agricultural societies obliged to exploit the land by scientific methods and to distribute the returns of labour among the co-operators according to a system of contract. In order to make possible a rational and scientific exploitation of the soil it is the duty of the State to spread, by means of technical schools and institutes, the necessary knowledge among the agricultural population."

As the Austrian Government had then commenced its action against the working-man Oberwinder, whom it accused of high treason, while Johann Most and the *Sozialdemokrat* still continued to accuse Liebknecht of being the tool of the Austrian Government, the following resolution was adopted amidst a storm of applause :—

"This Congress declares that the Austrian Government, in its attitude towards the Labour movement and its treatment of the incarcerated workmen, which is a mockery of all humanity, has earned the hatred and contempt of the workers of all nations."

The next Congress was to meet at Dresden in 1871.

When the elections to the Reichstag drew near, in 1870, Schweitzer's watchword was "Down with 'the honest men'!"—that is, the Social-Democratic Labour party. In the event of second ballots between our candidates and reactionaries, he recommended abstention, but in second ballots between our men and Liberals he recommended his followers to vote Liberal. We were greatly incensed by this infamous behaviour, and quite believed the statement that Schweitzer was acting under the orders of the Government, because our party was of all parties the most hostile to the Bismarckian policy. Yet notwithstanding this treachery we decided unanimously to support any candidate of any of the several Labour parties, with the personal exception of Schweitzer, who was to be opposed at Barmen-Elberfeld, in order to purge the Labour movement of a man who, under cover of Radicalism, had done all that was in his power to damage the movement.

In July both the *Sozialdemokrat* and our paper, the *Volksstaat,* were forced to announce a reduction in size ; the Franco-German War had suddenly broken out ; many of our readers had to rejoin the colours, while others were thrown out of employment.

As to the causes and the course of the war I shall have something to say later on. Liebknecht and I considered Napoleon and Bismarck equally to blame for the outbreak, and when the war-loan was voted we abstained, an attitude which we explained in a declaration published in the Journal of the Reichstag. But for Schweitzer the war was not merely a war against the German people, but a war against Socialism, and every German who fought against the peace-breakers was at the same time fighting against the arch-enemy of the ideas of the future, fighting for liberty, equality, and fraternity. Such was the prevailing state of excitement that the most bombastic fustian was believed, and was sufficient to arouse a prejudice against us.

In the midst of the war-fever came the news from Vienna of the condemnation of the Austrian workers who had taken part in the Eisenach Congress to long years of penal servitude and banishment. One of the condemned was Johann Most.

The entire Press attacked Liebknecht and myself on account of our behaviour in the Reichstag. The *Sozialdemokrat* was not behindhand, calling us traitors and worse. Schweitzer even sent emissaries to Leipzig to incite the masses against us. They met with no success. Once, while at a meeting, we were informed that the Schweitzerians had marched to Liebknecht's house in order to break the windows. We ran thither at the double, but arrived too late. Some windows had already

been smashed, greatly to the distress of Frau Liebknecht, who was just nursing her baby. We ran
off again angrily, and on overtaking the miscreants
gave them a sound drubbing. Some days later a
number of students had intended a similar ovation
for me, which was to be enlivened by a *Katzen-
musik* (cat's music, Charivari), but they were frus-
trated by my landlord, who locked the door of
the inner court above which I lodged.

All these attempts, and many others not worth
recording, so enraged my electors that they, poor
though they were, subscribed among themselves and
sent me a silver laurel wreath, accompanied by a
poem of Uhland's. Had I suspected their intention
I would have prevented its execution.

The *Sozialdemokrat* now suddenly executed a
volte-face. The strings which connected Schweitzer
with those in high places had evidently broken.
The war, with its uninterrupted series of victories,
had brought South Germany and almost the whole
of the middle classes of North Germany as well
to Bismarck's feet. Even in the ranks of South
German democracy Chauvinism was in the ascendant ; there was a veritable orgy of patriotism.
Bismarck could now dispense with men of
Schweitzer's stamp.

Thus the *Sozialdemokrat* wrote in disapproval
of the " compulsory annexation of Alsace-Lorraine,

and the reinstatement of Napoleon," just as we did in the *Volksstaat*.

When the executive of our party in Brunswick were arrested and sent in chains to the fortress of Lötzen, the *Sozialdemokrat* maliciously remarked : "Liebknecht and Bebel, the arch-instigators, are safe ; they send others to the firing-line." But it had not to wait very long to see its desire accomplished.

The Reichstag assembled again on the 24th of November. The *Sozialdemokrat* announced that the deputies of the party would vote against a further loan ; the war, originally a defensive campaign, had become a war of conquest. Here again Schweitzer approached our standpoint ; yet in all the debates on this subject which Liebknecht and I were constantly provoking, Schweitzer and his friends remained silent.

On the 17th of December Liebknecht and another editor of the *Volksstaat* and myself were suddenly arrested in our homes by the police, our rooms were searched, and we were taken into custody. We were thus paralysed during the elections ; but Schweitzer did not scruple to remind the members of his Union of their pledge to defeat the "honest men." And this when we were in prison, treated with the utmost severity, while the Public Prosecutor and the judges were concocting an indictment for high treason ! However, the Leipzig members of the General Union had too much common honesty and class-consciousness to take his part, but made common cause with our members, and put me up as their joint candidate for Leipzig.

On the 3rd of March, 1871, the *Sozialdemokrat* published a leader full of vainglorious boasting ; yet Schweitzer was beaten in the second ballot by the Conservative, the very man who in 1867 had contributed £60 towards Schweitzer's election expenses ! This defeat increased Schweitzer's inclination to retire from public life. He announced his irrevocable decision to retire from the presidency of the Union. Friends and opponents were equally surprised. He may have intended to resign eventually, but his real motive probably resided in the fact that he despaired of ever regaining the full confidence of the Union, which he had lost by so many acts of commission and omission, while he felt that his campaign against the Social-Democratic Labour party had no chance of permanent success. For our party, in spite of weakness of organisation and lack of unity, was gaining ground daily. The time was approaching when Schweitzer would have been forced to seek alliance with us, which would have meant the repudiation of all his previous tactics. He preferred to go of his own free will ; he had already prepared the way for his return to bourgeois society by the production, in January, 1871, of a three-act drama, "Canossa," which gave evidence of considerable dramatic power.

As early as April 30th a section of the Hatzfeldt organisation had resolved upon union with our party. At the General Meeting of the Labour Union held on the 19th of May Schweitzer announced that the *Sozialdemokrat* had ceased publication. It had never paid its way, he stated ; it had never even paid its editor's salary. The Union resolved to revive it under the title of the *Neue Sozialdemokrat*. Although Schweitzer was violently attacked in this very meeting, it eventually passed a unanimous vote of thanks for his energetic leadership of the party, and expressed its regret at learning of his retirement. But this unanimous vote of thanks was in violent contrast to the proceedings of the next meeting, which was held in 1872. Schweitzer was then accused, by a former confidant, of embezzling the money of the Union, and of being the confidential agent of the Berlin police. Finally Schweitzer, who was present at the meeting, was asked to leave, and a resolution was passed by 5,595 votes against 1,177 excluding him for ever from the Union.

This was the end of Schweitzer's political career. He was abandoned and condemned even by those who had for years given him their unbounded confidence. He was a man who must have remained the eminent leader of his party if to his other qualifications he had added those which are indispensable in a Labour leader : unselfishness, honesty, and complete devotion to the cause. He would then have been the right man in the right place, and many years of fierce and internecine conflict, in which time, money, health, and energy were squandered, to the satisfaction of our enemies, would have been avoided. It is to his credit that he had the faculty of spreading the ideas of Socialism among the masses, and of expressing them with a rare lucidity and vividness ; but his political double-dealing sowed the tares of fanaticism and discord among the workers and kept them permanently divided.

And it is my conviction that this was his real intention. The true purpose of his activities—in Bismarck's eyes the only purpose—was to create a Labour movement which should be subservient to the Government. There can be no doubt that Schweitzer was in Bismarck's service.

Schweitzer often complained of the ingratitude of the working-classes. This is quite consistent with the facts. He came into the movement with an erroneous conception of the part he was to play. The leader of a party becomes a real leader only by giving the party of his best, like an honest man ;

to give his best is the duty and obligation of any man who plays a part in the democratic movement. By his services he acquires the confidence of the masses, who accept him as their leader. But only as the man they most trust : not as a master whom they must blindly obey. He is the chosen protagonist of their demands, the interpreter of their longings, their hopes, and ambitions. So long as he is this the party accords him its confidence. But once the people see that they have been tricked and deceived, it is not only their right but their duty to deprive him of the leadership and of their confidence alike. The party does not exist for the leader, but the leader for the party. And as every position of authority contains the possibility of misuse, it is the duty of the party to control the actions of its leader and to supervise them.

Schweitzer saw things differently—upside-down, as it were. He saw himself as a kind of benefactor, and the party was to be the pedestal which he was to ascend, the means of satisfying his ambition and indulging his expensive tastes. When he did not succeed he complained of ingratitude. The masses are never ungrateful, so long as they have faith in the honesty of their leader ; and once they have given him their confidence it is not easy to convince them that they are being deceived.

History abounds in examples. Whoever accuses the masses of ingratitude should accuse himself, for the fault is his.

When Schweitzer had lost the game he suddenly recommended his friends of the Union to join our party ; that is, he recommended what he had fought against for all these years. He asked us to publish in the *Volksstaat* a manifesto to that effect. But we, suspecting a trap, refused. I think his action was prompted only by a desire to make things difficult for his successor in the presidency of the Union. For at this time, while he was asking us to publish his manifesto, a farce of his was produced, entitled " Our Great Citizen," in which the chief actors in the General German Labour Union were mercilessly caricatured and derided. Even the bourgeois Press censured him severely for this breach of good taste.

Schweitzer died on the 28th of July, 1875, of tuberculosis. He was buried in the family vault in Frankfort. None of his former admirers and supporters followed the hearse. For the Social-Democrats he was extinct before he died. There were no obituaries to testify that the former leader was not quite forgotten. This was the end of one of the most remarkable leaders of the German Labour movement, an end for which no one but himself was to blame.

CHAPTER XIII

IN PARLIAMENT

1. The North German Constituent Reichstag.

As soon as the official confirmation of my election to the Reichstag was in my pocket, I started for Berlin, on the 5th of March, 1867, not without a certain palpitation of the heart. The Session had opened on the 24th of February. I was about to enter upon political activities of quite a new kind ; I was a total stranger to parliamentary life, and had no one to introduce me or initiate me. My colleague, Schraps, a barrister, was no better off in this respect. But I had to take the plunge. When I went to the Chamber and was about to open the door, it was suddenly opened from the inside, and out came Prince Frederick Charles, who was a member—a meeting of the two extremes on the social scale. Having handed in my paper to the Secretary, I went to call on some people to whom I had introductions from a friend at Leipzig. They complained of the Prussian

supporters of the party—they belonged to the
Progressive party—the best among them being
unable to rise to a really free and democratic
ideal.

I was assigned to the first division—that is, I
became a member of the first of the seven divisions
into which the Chamber was divided, for business
reasons. This is why the numbers of the com-
mittees composed by members of the Reichstag
must always be divisible by seven.

About this time I wrote to my wife : " W., my
colleague, and I form the extreme Left of the
Reichstag, and our seats are placed accordingly.
We cannot well move farther to the left on account
of the walls, for we do not intend to run our heads
against them."

The Deputies at this time included the fine flower
of the North German politicians ; von Bennigsen,
who had presided over the previous year's meeting of delegates at Frankfort ; Dr. Karl Braun,
of Wiesbaden, the licensed jester of the Chamber,
known also for a famous connoisseur of vintages ;
the red-headed Becker, whom I knew of old ; Max
Duncker, proud of his " lion's mane " ; von
Forckenbeck, who was to become President after
Simson, and the most prejudiced President the
Chamber ever knew ; Gustav Freytag, the well-
known novelist ; Rudolf von Gneist, whom the

Minister of War, von Roon, once paid the doubtful compliment of saying that he was a man who could prove anything and everything ; little Lasker, who used to look like a weasel as he ran to the rostrum with his short little legs ; Dr. Planck, later on the principal draughtsman of the German Civil Code ; Eugen Richter, still as sour-looking as when I first knew him in Frankfort, in 1863 ; Dr. Simson, once President of the Frankfort Parliament, now first President of the Reichstag, whose dignified manner as he presided or rang his bell earned him the sobriquet of Jupiter Tonans ; von Schwerin, once a Minister in a Prussian Liberal Ministry, who gave his name to the so-called " Schwerinstage "—the days, usually Wednesdays, reserved for the motions of private Members ; the well-known supporter of co-operation, Schulze-Delitzsch ; Twesten, celebrated for his duel with von Mannteufel ; von Unruh, a Liberal *Junker;* Waldeck, the real leader of the Progressives ; Windthorst und Malinckrodt, future leaders of the Centre ; and Privy Councillor Wagener, the real leader of the Conservatives, and confidant of Bismarck.

Another personage of some importance in the Reichstag was Karl Mayer von Rothschild, the Member for Frankfort, which had been annexed after 1866. He was a squat, broad-shouldered man, with

well-groomed jet-black hair and beard ; he wore
a heavy gold chain over his ample paunch, and
was always most elegantly dressed. I recognised
him at once, although I had never seen his por-
trait. There were also two generals among the
Deputies—Vogel von Falckenstein and von Stein-
metz, who were elected in recognition of their
victories in the Austrian campaign of 1866.

But above all these I was interested in Bismarck,
whom I had never seen before. He almost always
attended the Reichstag wearing a black frock-coat,
a black waistcoat, and a black stock so high that
only the narrowest rim of white collar was visible
above it. His hair, or as much as was left of it,
was dark, as was his moustache. I looked in vain
for the famous triad of hairs standing upright, like
poplars on a plain, in the midst of an otherwise
bald cranium, as shown in all the caricatures. I
was very anxious to hear him speak, and was
greatly disappointed to find that, giant though he
was, he did not roar like a lion or speak with the
voice of Stentor ; his voice was actually a high
treble. He made use of long and involved sentences, and was sometimes hesitating, but all he
said was of interest and to the point.

Although Bismarck had made his peace with the
Liberals, he still feared their parliamentary in-
stability, and had devised the Constitution accord-

ingly. He made some slight concessions to them, but remained firm upon two points : no payment of Members, and the establishment of the Military Budget on the Consolidated Fund. But he defended universal suffrage, which was proposed for the Constitution, against the attacks of the National Liberals. Sybel, the historian, declared that universal suffrage would mean the tyranny of democracy. Bismarck, on the contrary, said he knew of no better electoral system. It was a sort of heirloom to us Germans, a legacy from the struggles for German unity ; it was part and parcel of the Constitution of the Empire adopted at Frankfort ; it was proposed by Prussia in opposition to the Austrian proposals of 1863. No other common basis was possible in a league of twenty-one States. The three-class system he regarded as the *most miserable and illogical electoral system imaginable*.

My first action in Parliament was to induce the Chamber to commit an illegal action. In one of the first Sessions of the division (committee) to which I belonged, the election of the Member for Leipzig was to be verified. Now, the Town Council of Leipzig, who were responsible for the electoral arrangements, and had to keep the registers, had committed some irregularity which should have rendered the election void. I made a speech in which I asserted that even if the irregularities had not occurred, the candidate would have been elected (it was simply a question of distributing the electors over the various electoral districts). So much I could say from my six-years experience of the political conditions of the city. My view, although absolutely illegal, was adopted, and the election was declared valid. Such a thing could, of course, only happen while affairs were in a state of unstable equilibrium, as they were during the first Session of the new Chamber.

Of course, I had the most ardent desire to make a speech during a full-dress debate, and numerous appeals to the same effect reached me from my constituency. Although I could not, on account of the closure, speak in the debate on the First Reading of the Constitution Act, I was at last able to make my speech on the 14th Article, which dealt with the relation of the North German Confederation to the States of South Germany. In my speech I attacked the policy of Prussia, and maintained, in the face of many interruptions, that the unification of Germany, as intended by Prussia, was not in the interests of Germany as a whole, but only in those of a Greater Prussia, and the Hohenzollern Dynasty. Prussia did not want the South German States to enter the Confederation, because it was feared that the Prussian Government might be outvoted. Such a policy, I added, was not a German policy ; it would not result in unification, but the disruption of Germany. It would turn Germany into one great military barracks, and destroy the last remains of liberty and popular rights.

In the debate that followed we were denounced for our support of the South and as allies of the Ultramontane party—that is, the new Centre—and these denunciations continue to the present day.

My maiden speech made a considerable stir, both inside and outside the House. It greatly pleased my constituents. The *Gartenlaube* was then publishing a series of articles on " Remarkable Personalities in the Reichstag " ; I was accorded the honour of a particular mention in these articles, the author saying of my speech that " it was as if the throbbing of the wings of the stormy petrel of revolution was heard throughout the House." This seemed to the editor to be praise of an indiscreet or extravagant kind ; the number was withdrawn from circulation, and the phrase was altered.

My opening speech had yet another sequel. Some weeks later two gentlemen of aristocratic appearance came to my workshop while I was at work. They asked for Bebel, the master-turner. When I replied that I was Bebel, they looked at me in some surprise, one of them saying, "I mean Deputy Bebel." I repeated, a little piqued, that I was Bebel; he surveyed me from top to toe, and gave his name as Baron von Friesen. He was the brother of the Saxon Minister. He had read my speech, and was delighted with certain portions thereof; I thanked him for his compliments. The Particularists of that time were animated by the most ungovernable hatred of Bismarck; they would have entered into an alliance with the devil in order to destroy him.

Towards the end of the Session the King invited the entire Reichstag to a banquet in the palace. Liebknecht, myself, and certain others did not attend. Next morning I met my good friend the red-headed Becker, and asked him: "Well, Becker, how did you enjoy your dinner-party at Wilhelm's?"

He laid both hands on my shoulders—I think he was still a trifle vinous—and replied: "Magnificent, my dear Bebel! Such delicious wines, and a fellow behind you who fills your glass as soon as it is empty!"

I laughingly asked him: "Then I suppose you will accept the invitation to the palace?"

"Well, my friend, you may be sure of that!"

Now, Becker and Miquel had in their youth been members of the Communist League. Some of the members of this league had quite notable careers ; Miquel became Chief Magistrate of Frankfort, and later Prussian Minister of Finance, and was finally ennobled. Becker became Chief Magistrate of Cologne and a member of the Prussian House of Peers. Others were equally successful.

We, as well as the Radicals (Progressives), voted against the Constitution Act, which was, however, passed into law by a majority of 230 votes against 53. We took this course because it did not give the representatives of the people the rights to which they were entitled. It contained no fundamental or organic laws, no rights of the purse, no ministerial responsibility, no payment of Members. On the other hand, it settled the Army Budget on the Consolidated Fund, and gave too great a share of power to the Chancellor of the Confederation, who, from 1871, became the Chancellor of the Empire.

At the close of the Session I made a tour of my constituency, in order to speak at various meetings, and report to my constituents on the work of the Session and the part I had taken in it. The meetings were very well attended, and I was much interested in the fact that from the very outset women constituted a not inconsiderable portion of my audiences. These women became most zealous agitators. As we had no newspapers at our disposal, these meetings were an absolute necessity. I continued this work after the close of every Session, and gradually succeeded in building up relations of mutual confidence between my electors and myself that stood me in such good stead that my opponents were never able to oust me from my seat. When, after ten years, I had, for tactical reasons, to change my constituency, I did so with great regret.

2. THE NORTH GERMAN REICHSTAG AND THE CUSTOMS DIET.

The first session of the first North German Reichstag opened on the 10th of September, 1867. Among the new Deputies were Barons von Hoverbeck and von Kirchmann. Each had a democratic record, and each belonged to the Radical party. Von Kirchmann had been a Prussian judge, holding a high position, from which he was dismissed on account of the " immorality " of a lecture given by him, in which he advocated the voluntary limitation of the birth-rate, in the interests of the higher development of civilisation. Field-Marshal von Moltke was also a Deputy ; so was the famous Strousberg, the notorious company-promoter, who contrived to get the most aristocratic names on his prospectuses. He was the typical parvenu. His parties made a sensation by their extravagance, and received columns of description in the Press, a thing hitherto unknown in Berlin. It was the era of capitalism with a big " C " that Strousberg's advent announced—the unholy union of aristocracy with plutocracy.

My first speech was on the Address. I protested that the Reichstag had no right to call itself the representative of the German nation. Ten millions of Germans in Austria and eight millions in South Germany, to say nothing of Luxemburgh, had been sacrificed. Bismarck interrupted me by asking whether I would have gone to war with France for the sake of Luxemburgh. I, of course, answered in the negative, but that Luxemburgh had been sacrificed to Napoleon ; its retention would have been of great political value to Germany, for, as the Grand Duke of Luxemburgh was also King of Holland, it would have bound the latter country firmly to Germany, which would have been a great advantage in all international complications.

My second speech was in connection with the law of universal military service. As it was impossible, on account of the great expense, to enrol all citizens capable of bearing arms while the term of service was at all protracted—it was then three years with the colours—I asked for a return to the system introduced by Scharnhorst and Gneisenau, proposing a term of nine months with the colours.

Our proposals were, of course, rejected, but I received many congratulatory communications from all parts of Germany. Our Leipzig friends sent us a token of their approval in the shape of a nine-pound ham, which was very welcome to unsalaried members as we then were.

The Session was adjourned in the spring of 1868, in order to make room for a session of the Customs Diet, which was to sit for the first time in Berlin, on the 27th of April. The people responsible for the distribution of seats had—rather disingenuously and maliciously—placed Rothschild side by side with Liebknecht. The House roared with laughter ; but Rothschild soon deserted this dangerous neighbourhood and had another seat allotted to him.

The majority of the South German Deputies found it extremely difficult to resign themselves to the new order of things. The Customs Diet was the outcome of the fratricidal war of 1866, and South Germany was still suffering from the wounds then inflicted. The feeling of defeat had not yet vanished. Moreover, the Diet was a makeshift, being neither flesh nor fish. The Liberals, as the representatives of capitalistic development, wanted to make the Diet a true German Parliament ; a measure resisted by Bismarck on the grounds of French jealousy and the state of feeling in the south, and also by the other parties of South

Germany, who did not recognise their cherished ideal in the North German Confederation, with its Constitution and its Customs Duties. The antagonism between North and South was still so keen that the people of the South knew more of Vienna and Paris than of Berlin, which they rarely visited. In the debates this antagonism often gave rise to violent altercations. But here, as elsewhere, it was proved that the South German is no match for the North German in tenacity and determination. Liebknecht and I did our utmost to stiffen the backbones of the South German Deputies, whose political principles were more akin to ours than to those of the North. Most of the South Germans were glad to turn their backs upon Berlin after four weeks of unremunerated attendance. (In most of the South German States the Deputies were salaried.) The sittings were, as a rule, very poorly attended.

The next Session of the North German Reichstag —in 1869—was chiefly devoted to a new code for the regulation of trade and industry. I spoke on several occasions, attacking Privy Councillor Wagener as the Royal Prussian Court Socialist, and defending our propaganda and organisation against the attacks of Baron von Stumm,* maintaining that

* A great ironmaster, known for his violent attacks on Social-Democracy.

as the organisation of capitalism was international, that of labour must be the same.

At this point I should like to say something of the sacrifices which our participation in the debates of the Reichstag and the Customs Diet imposed upon us. Our constituents—it is only fair to them to say it—did their best to help us financially, but it was very painful to us to accept assistance from those whom we knew to be among the poorest of the electorate. The party paid us nothing ; it had not the means earlier than 1878, and then it could afford only a meagre pittance. We had to pay even our travelling expenses to and from Berlin out of our own pockets. We thus missed many sittings, even when our presence was of the greatest importance to our party. It was the same with the other parties. The majority of the Bills passed were passed by Houses which did not contain a quorum. This state of things continued until 1906, when salaries were finally granted.

In the same Session the electoral law was passed. The Lassalleans had brought in an amendment fixing the age limit at twenty-one instead of twenty-five, and establishing Sunday as election day. I moved that the elections should be fixed for the whole Confederation on one and the same day, that day to be a Sunday or other holiday, and that there should be no disqualification of paupers. Of course, all our amendments were rejected. But at the instance of the National Liberals all electors serving with the colours at the time of an election were disqualified.

In the debates on the Budget Baron von Hoverbeck had advocated disarmament. I objected, saying that it was folly to think of disarmament as matters then stood in Europe, while Cæsarism was rampant both within the country and without, and one Cæsar was only awaiting the opportunity to attack and destroy the other. It was like the story of the two lions in the fable, who devoured one another until only the tails were left. When that stage was reached our turn would come.

In the Reichstag of 1870 I spoke against the death penalty. It had been abolished in Saxony and in Baden ; but Bismarck insisted upon it, and it was included in the new Criminal Code by a majority of 27 votes (137 against 110).

The Customs Diet of 1870 sat only for three weeks. A Bavarian Deputy—a Progressive—resigned, stating as his motive that the Diet was a sham, which existed only to increase the power of Prussia. It is remarkable how tame and shy of fighting the bourgeois party—the Democrats—had gradually become, quite oblivious of the fact that it is only by fighting that a party can live and grow. The more intelligent had begun to understand that in view of the developments of Social-Democracy, bourgeois democracy had no future. An ever-increasing class antagonism was widening the rift between the sheep and the goats.

The Spring Session of the Customs Diet of 1870 was to be its last ; a few months later commenced the great tragedy which completely altered the political conditions of Germany and made a Customs Diet superfluous.

Between Liebknecht and myself there existed some differences of opinion as to the tactics which our party should adopt in the Reichstag. Liebknecht regarded the North German Confederation as a thing to be fought against with any and every means available, until it was utterly destroyed. To take any part in its Assembly, otherwise than by way of protest and absolute negation, was in his eyes a betrayal of the revolutionary ideal. No truckling, therefore, to compromise and arrangement ; no attempts to influence legislation in our favour !

I did not share this conception of the revolutionary ideal. I was for protest and denial whenever they were necessary, especially protest against all that was pernicious from our point of view ; but I was also in favour of positive action, such as the moving of amendments of a propagandist nature. Then our speeches were bound to reach millions of readers, however much the reports might be bowdlerised by the Press, and to spread and plead for our principles.

These differences as to tactics came to a head during the Session, and Liebknecht finally felt bound to state his position. This he did in a lecture delivered before the Berlin Democratic Labour Society, which was afterwards published in pamphlet form. In this he stated his belief that Socialism was not a matter of theory but of power, and a question that could not be solved in Parliament but only in the open, on the field of battle, as all other questions of power had to be settled. To make speeches in the Reichstag was useless ; and to make useless speeches was the work of fools. " No peace," he said, " in the existing State."

This purely negative attitude was never that of the party as a whole. When, later on, under the laws directed against Socialism, Anarchism obtained a hold here and there in Germany, the anarchists, of course, used Liebknecht's pamphlet against us, the " Parliamentarian party." This was insupportable ; so Liebknecht loyally agreed to publish a new edition of the pamphlet, stating in an introduction that his remarks were intended to apply only to political conditions in Germany before the foundation of the Empire (1871). Later, at a Congress at St. Gall, held in 1887, he openly and frankly declared that he had been converted to my point of view and that he regarded the practical participation of the party in parliamentary life as necessary and of the greatest advantage to the party.

CHAPTER XIV

THE FRANCO-GERMAN WAR .

1. Preliminaries to the Declaration of War.

The attitude which Liebknecht and I assumed at
the outbreak of the war and maintained throughout
the course of it, both within the Reichstag and
without, has for years been the subject of discussion and the occasion of violent attacks upon us.
This was the case, too, within our own party for a
time, though not for long, as we were soon seen to be
in the right. I can assert that I do not in any way
regret the attitude we then adopted, and that had
we at the outbreak of the war known all that afterwards became known, whether from official or
other publications, our attitude would have been
even more hostile to the war from the very outset.
Not only should we have abstained from voting ;
we should even have voted against the first grants
of money.

To-day there can be no doubt that the war of

1870 was desired by Bismarck, and that he had long laid his plans to bring it about. Although in respect of the wars of 1864 and 1866 his pose as the innocent victim, the party attacked, was hardly successful, the same could not be said of the war of 1870, when his pose was brilliantly maintained. With the exception of a small inner circle of intimates who knew that Bismarck had worked with might and main to bring about the war—and not even the then King of Prussia, Wilhelm I., belonged to this inner circle—Bismarck duped the whole world, making every one believe that Napoleon had provoked the war, while poor, peace-loving Bismarck was the aggrieved party. The semi-official and official historians have fostered this belief among the general masses of the population, according to which Germany was acting on the defensive and France was the attacking party. It is true that Napoleon declared war, but the admirable point in Bismarck's policy was that he so shuffled the cards that Napoleon was forced to declare war as though of his own initiative and to appear as the peacebreaker.

Even men like Marx and Engels shared the common opinion, and gave public expression thereto, although in their position they ought to have known better. The events that preceded the declaration of the war were so confusing and unexpected that people quite overlooked the fact that France, who declared war, was quite unprepared, while Germany had all her preparations completed to the last button, and succeeded in mobilising her forces without the slightest hitch.

I first accused Bismarck of having provoked the war in two articles published in the *Volksstaat* of 1873, entitled " The Second of September," * in which I gave an account of the now famous telegram of Ems which made the war inevitable.

In these matters Liebknecht and I did not see eye to eye. He was of the opinion that Napoleon desired the war, but that Bismarck had not the courage to take up the challenge. Thus he wrote on the 16th of July : " The courageous party retreats—before the stronger. The Hohenzollern candidature † has been abandoned in consequence of the threatening attitude of Bonaparte ; peace will be preserved and the mighty North German Confederation, which was to make Germany respected abroad, has hauled down its colours

---

* The 2nd of September is the anniversary of the capitulation of Sedan, when Napoleon and a French army of some 120,000 men were taken prisoners.

† A Prince of Hohenzollern blood had been invited by the Government of Spain to ascend the throne. This Napoleon resented, and asked the King of Prussia to veto the proposal as head of the Hohenzollerns.

as humbly as it did in the Luxemburg affair." *

I was of a different opinion, being convinced that Napoleon had fallen into a trap prepared for him by Bismarck. I was greatly incensed with Liebknecht, and high words passed between us ; but we were soon reconciled, and from the 20th of July and onwards the *Volksstaat* adopted my views.

Knowing nothing of the imminence of war, we had called a party meeting for the 17th of July. Now we had to define our attitude towards the war, and did so in the following resolution :—

" This meeting protests against any war but one undertaken in the interests of freedom and civilisation, as a crime against modern civilisation. This meeting protests against a war waged in the interests of a dynasty, which jeopardises the lives of hundreds of thousands and the welfare of millions in order to satisfy the ambition of a few of those in power. This meeting hails with joy the attitude of the French democracy, especially of the socialistic workers, and declares its complete

* In 1867, after the dissolution of the Germanic Confederation, Napoleon objected to the Prussian garrison. Prussia refused to give way. But a conference sitting in London agreed upon the neutrality of Luxemburgh, the withdrawal of the Prussian garrison, and the dismantling of the fortress.

sympathy with their efforts to prevent the war, and expects the German democracy and German workers to uplift their voices for the same purpose."

The workers of Paris declared against the war before we did so. Similar resolutions were passed by public meetings of working-men in many cities, such as Barmen, Berlin, Nürnberg, Augsburg, Munich, Königsberg, Fürth, Krefeld, &c.

The party executive in Brunswick was of a different opinion. It convened a public meeting for the 16th of July, which passed a resolution to the effect that as France and a majority of the representatives of the French people had frivolously broken the peace of Europe, and as the German nation was the party aggrieved and attacked, the meeting regarded the defensive war as an unavoidable evil, but asked the whole people to do their utmost to induce the German people to decide in fullest sovereignty upon the question of peace or war. Similar resolutions were passed in many cities, especially in the North. Thus a very definite difference of opinion within the party became apparent.

The Reichstag was to be opened on the 19th of July. Liebknecht considered it was our duty to vote against any war loan. But it was thought that a vote against the loan would be a vote in favour of Napoleon. The only possible course was for us to abstain from voting. Liebknecht finally agreed to this, and to justify our action we had the following declaration inserted in the Journal of the Reichstag :—

" The present war is a dynastic war in the interest of the Bonaparte dynasty, as the war of 1866 was in the interest of the Hohenzollern dynasty.

" We cannot vote the moneys required for the conduct of this war, as this would imply a vote of confidence in the Prussian Government, which prepared the way for this war by its proceedings in 1866.

" Neither can we vote in an adverse sense, as that would be equivalent to approval of the wicked and criminal policy of Bonaparte.

" As we are in principle opposed to all dynastic wars, and as Socialist Republicans and members of the International Association of Labour, which, without regard for nationality, opposes all oppressors and strives to unite in one fraternal union all the oppressed, cannot, either directly or indirectly, declare for the present war, we therefore abstain from voting, in the confident hope that the peoples of Europe, taught by the present fateful events, will do everything to conquer their rights of self-direction, and to abolish the existing supremacy of class and the sword, which is the cause of all public and social evil."

The loan, amounting to some £18,000,000, was, of course, voted. The Lassalleans gave their votes in favour of it. But the German capitalists afforded the world a sorry spectacle. Although the interest on the loan was 5 per cent. and the price of issue only 88, only some £10,000,000 of the amount was subscribed, while in France the £28,000,000 of the French War Loan was applied for in full. So much for the patriotism of the German capitalists !

Our attitude in the Reichstag widened the difference between us and the party committee. Liebknecht refused to edit the *Volksstaat* according to the wishes of the committee, and was finally so far angered that he threatend to emigrate, so greatly did "this nationalist paroxysm disgust him." I, too, greatly objected to the admonitions of the committee, and wrote to them informing them that I should refuse to write for the *Volksstaat* if they proceeded against Liebknecht. In answer to their reproach that we acted as we did merely from motives of what they called our "Saxon particularism," * I maintained that we Saxons were good Socialist Republicans.

On the 1st of September Liebknecht wrote to a

* Particularists are sticklers for State rights, especially as opposed to Prussian preponderance.

correspondent: "I should not give up my position because I am afraid of these place-hunters, but because I am disgusted with their patriotic frenzy. This malady must run its course; meanwhile I am superfluous here, and could be very useful elsewhere—for example, in America. But I still hope it will soon be over, so that I need not go away."

The course of events forced him to stay and take up his position in the forefront of the battle.

2. The Arrest of the Party Committee at Brunswick.

On the 30th of June the Committee published in the *Volksstaat* a manifesto in which the differences which still divided us became apparent. "It is our task," they said, "to play a decisive part at the birth of this new State, which, as we hope, will embrace the whole of Germany, so that it may result, not in a dynastic but in a Social-Democratic Commonwealth. It is our task to imprint upon it the stamp of our ideas in a sharp and bitter struggle if at its birth the new State still wears dynastic colours. They hoped for the victory of our arms over France, but hoped the victors would not give themselves over to vaingloriousness. The fratricidal war between two countries was to be regretted, but it was not the fault of Germany. The guilty would receive their just punishment, but this once achieved it would be a question of uniting forces for the glorious common struggle of all the oppressed of the earth. With Napoleon vanquished the French people would breathe freely once more, and we Germans would call upon our rulers to give the people their due and what the immense sacrifices and miseries of the war would entitle them rightfully to demand."

The members of the Committee in their optimism did not suspect that they would be the first victims of the " glorious victory." The French armies were utterly defeated, by rapid blows, and Germany soon had whole armies of prisoners captive, whose housing and feeding became a very disagreeable burden. Then came the Battle of Sedan, which Napoleon accepted under such circumstances as made it clear that he did so purposely, preferring to become the prisoner of Germany rather than return to France a beaten man. When the news of his surrender reached Germany, every one was jubilant. All thought it would mean the end of a war which had already become a matter of general disgust, on account of the immense losses suffered. Even the King of Prussia wrote to his wife: " I am afraid to inquire as to the losses."

Yet the war was continued. Paris responded to the capture of Napoleon by proclaiming a Republic, a coup which was far from welcome to those at the German headquarters. Assuredly the war had not been undertaken in order to convert France into a Republic ! This, it was feared—though without cause—would prove a bad example. When the news of the proclamation of the Republic reached Germany, Liebknecht, greatly excited, with tears in his eyes, rushed into my workshop to announce the event. He was much taken aback by the cool indifference with which I received the news. But to the committee also this news came like a bolt from the blue, and effected a rapid change of feeling. All differences vanished on the instant. We were in complete accord, and demanded the immediate conclusion of peace, the imposition of a war indemnity, but no annexation. Yet what had been a defensive war had become a war of conquest.

On the 7th of August the General Council of the " International " published a manifesto, which was printed in the *Volksstaat*. It declared the war to be a dynastic war on the part of Napoleon, and defensive on the part of Germany. " But," it continued, " if the German workers permit it to lose its defensive character and to degenerate into a war against the French people, victory or defeat will be equally fatal. Prussia alone would reap the advantage."

The committee, acting on this manifesto, pub-

lished a proclamation "To All German Workers."
It asked the workers to assist the efforts of the
Republican French Government to obtain an
honourable peace. It quoted from a letter of
Marx—though his name was not mentioned—a
passage to the effect that the war of 1870 would
necessarily be followed by another between
Germany and Russia, and that the centre of
gravity of the Labour movement would shift from
France to Germany. The German workers ought
to show their consciousness of their great responsibility, and agitate, by means of public meetings,
against the annexation of Alsace-Lorraine, and for
a speedy and honourable peace with the French
Republic. The proclamation concluded: "When
we see that a great people has once again
taken its destinies into its own hands, and that
Republics exist, not only in Switzerland and over-
sea but *de facto* in France and Spain, let us join
in the cry which, if not to-day, yet perhaps on
some future date, will greet the dawn of freedom
even in Germany: the jubilant cry—Long live the
Republic!"

This proclamation was published on the 11th
of September. On the 14th we had to announce
that General Vogel von Falkenstein, who held command in North Germany, being detailed to prevent
the French from landing on the German coast,

had given the order—in defiance of law and justice, as afterwards appeared—to put the Party Committee in chains and transport them, with a strong military escort, to Lötzen, a fortress in Eastern Prussia, where they were to be imprisoned. The prisoners were very brutally treated ; thus the journey to Königsberg took thirty-six hours. On the way the people regarded them as traitors to their country and behaved accordingly.

Another of our party, who was named in our address, was also arrested. The same fate befell two Liberal Democrats, Johann Jacoby and Herbig. The arrest of these latter made a very bad impression on the Liberal Press. A Radical paper said at the time : " These arrests do not go well with our great victories, and make us wonder whether the German people will not lose in internal freedom what it has gained in external glory."

We, of course, were not surprised. We had not shared the illusion of our committee, which expected a Liberal development of the new order from the very man—Bismarck—who had been the arch-enemy of every liberal, not to say democratic development, and who now, as victor, placed his spurred boot on the neck of the new Empire.

Other members of our party were arrested for distributing the party manifesto. The Saxon Government prohibited all public meetings, in view of the final result of the war. Yet our party was very successful in the elections to the Town Councils of two Saxon towns—a fact which gave us some consolation.

The official *Norddeutsche Allgemeine Zeitung* regretted that Liebknecht and I had not been arrested with the committee. They had not long to wait.

A provisional committee was formed, with its headquarters at Dresden. As a good deal of correspondence was seized at the time of the arrest of the committee, I wrote warning the secretary not to keep any letters—a warning which he promptly disregarded. When, later on, a search was made of his premises, even my letter of advice fell into the hands of the police, and later still appeared in the records of the action for high treason which was brought against me.

A curious adventure befell Liebknecht and myself towards the end of October. The thirty-first of that month is a holiday in Saxony—the so-called Day of the Reformation—the anniversary of the day on which Luther affixed his ninety-five theses to the door of the church at Wittenberg. Two days before that date I received a registered letter, which urgently summoned Liebknecht and myself to proceed on some important business to Mittweida, a small Saxon town, on the 31st. We complied with this request. At the station we were met in the most mysterious manner, and were led, by a roundabout way, to a hotel, where, to our utmost surprise, we found assembled all the confidential party agents of the district. The question was put to us : Why did we remain inactive? Why did we not give the signal of insurrection while the army was away, while that portion of it remaining in the country could be easily overpowered? We shook our heads at this simplicity. I spoke to the meeting, demonstrating the absurdity of this demand ; Liebknecht, of course, did the same. It was not difficult to convince those present of the justice of our point of view. They, too, had come to Mittweida on the invitation of two comrades, without in the least suspecting what was in the wind.

3. Annexation of Alsace-Lorraine—The Empire.

After the capitulation of Sedan the war continued with undiminished vigour. The Imperial Army was destroyed and captured, but the Government of National Defence, with Gambetta and Freycinet at its head, succeeded in organising new armies. While the war against the Empire lasted only six weeks, the war against the Republic was to last six months. Most of our imprisoned comrades were released. The Party Committee, once more in chains, was brought back to Brunswick to undergo trial for high treason.

On the 24th of November the North German Reichstag was to meet in extraordinary session. The session was short, but very stirring. The motions before the House dealt with war loans for the continuation of the war, the treaties with the South German States concluded at Versailles, and the new Constitution of the Empire.

What had leaked out concerning these treaties had greatly displeased the Liberals. The South German States—Bavaria in particular—had insisted upon certain reservations, which greatly complicated the unity of the Empire. The North German Constitution was to become, with certain modifications, the Constitution of the Empire. There was little Liberalism or liberty in it. It did not even grant the payment of deputies. Moreover, people were depressed by the fact that the end of a war which had cost such enormous sacrifices was not yet in view.

On the 26th of November the motion of a further war loan of some £15,000,000 was the order of the day. I spoke against the motion; it was not a long speech, but it raised a storm the like of which no other speech of mine, before or after, ever produced. I maintained that as Napoleon was a prisoner the cause of the war had disappeared.

I quoted, amidst great commotion and protest, in
corroboration of my contention, the Speech from
the Throne and the proclamation of the King of
Prussia, which had referred to the war, not as
a war against the French people but merely against
Napoleon and his armies.

The great obstacle to a speedy conclusion of
peace was the policy of annexation. When I
alluded to the pitiful part the German capitalist
classes had played in connection with the War Loan
the storm increased. A large part of the House
was attacked by a kind of frenzy ; we were treated
to invective of the most offensive kind, while dozens
of Members rushed at us with clenched fists and
threatened to turn us out. For many minutes I
could not finish my speech. Finally I moved a
resolution embodying the chief points of my
speech refusing the loan, and especially recommending the speedy conclusion of peace and the
renunciation of all proposals to annex French territory. Liebknecht also spoke, laying especial stress
on the fact that annexation would bring, not peace
but war, and would perpetuate the danger of war.
Our resolution was, of course, negatived, five votes
being cast in its favour.

A few days later there was a Liberal inter-
pellation in the Prussian Diet in respect of the
imprisonment of Jacoby, a Liberal. Jacoby had

complained directly to Bismarck at Versailles.
Bismarck indirectly admitted Jacoby to be in the
right, but took no action. As we know from the
journal of his journalist-in-ordinary, Moritz Busch,
he was afraid of the military party at headquarters, and was greatly exasperated by the service
element, which spoiled his political plans.

During the Session of the 3rd of December I
complained of the treatment meted out to the committee. Miquel, on the contrary, justified these
arrests, maintaining that France was encouraged
to further resistance by our attitude—a contention
the untruth of which I immediately proved.

During one of the following Sessions the separate
treaties with the South German States were discussed. I spoke against these, as well as against
the new Constitution as a whole, as not conforming to the expectations of the German people in
the matter of liberty and unity. The three wars
of the last ten years had, from a Liberal standpoint, set Germany back. But the people would
assert their independence and give themselves the
only Constitution worth having—namely, a Republic.

Privy Councillor Wagener spoke after me, and,
to the great surprise of Liebknecht and myself,
quoted from a newspaper he had just received
passages of a letter which the French Consul at
Vienna had addressed to us, thanking us, in the

name of the French Republic, for our attitude in
the Reichstag. Amid cries of "Shame!" from all
sides of the Chamber I could only state that we
had never received such a letter, which was all
the more incomprehensible as the *Norddeutsche
Allgemeine Zeitung* had printed it. I stated my
opinion that the letter was a miserable concoction,
probably fabricated by the Press Bureau with the
intent to injure us. At the next sitting Wagener
maintained the letter to be genuine. I held to my
first declaration that I had received no such letter.
But at last I really did get it ; it was addressed
to Liebknecht and myself, and dated the 2nd of
December ; it had thus taken six days to reach
me. The letter was as follows :—

"GENTLEMEN,—In the name of the French Republic, the Government of which has appointed me
special envoy to the German democracy, I think
it my duty to thank you for the noble words you
have uttered in the Berlin Parliament, in the midst
of an assembly fanaticised by the spirit of conquest and the intoxication of militarism. The
courage you evinced on that occasion has attracted
the attention of all Europe, and has won for you
a glorious position in the ranks of the soldiers of
freedom. The liberal and humanitarian spirit of
Germany is suffering for the moment, as you,

gentlemen, have so eloquently asserted, one of those eclipses such as we ourselves have passed through, during the period of our First Empire, and will suffer the same disillusions. A frenzy of brutal domination has seized upon the most enlightened minds. Those thinkers who but a short time since emitted such brilliant rays of light all over the world have become, under the inspiration of Herr von Bismarck, the apostles of the murder and destruction of a whole nation. You, gentlemen, and your party, in the midst of this general desertion, maintain the great Germanic traditions. In our eyes you are the great representatives of the German nation, which we embrace with a truly fraternal affection, and have never ceased to love. France salutes you, sirs, and thanks you, for she beholds in you the future of Germany and the hope of a reconciliation of the two peoples."

This letter may have been well meant, but it was, at the moment, extremely untimely. We do not know who gave it to the newspapers. I suspect the letter was suggested to the Consul by some person or persons who wished to injure us.

On the 10th of December a deputation was appointed to present to the King, at Versailles, an address from the Reichstag congratulating him on the assumption of the dignity of Emperor. The

Progressive party, the majority of which had voted with us against the Constitution, had refused to participate in the address. The members of the deputation were to be selected by lot. We said not a word, but took our chances. Had we been allotted we should of course have declined. But we escaped. When the name of Rothschild was read out Windthorst—the leader of what was afterwards the party of the Centre—went solemnly up to him, shook him vigorously by the hand, and congratulated him. The whole House shook with laughter.

After the close of the Session we returned to Leipzig, and on the 15th of December gave an account of the debates at a public meeting of the Social-Democratic Labour party. The audience was so large that it was a real assembly of the people. Amidst the audience were many French officers in mufti, who, as prisoners of war, had been assigned to Leipzig. The meeting passed a resolution enthusiastically approving our attitude in the Reichstag. This was our last public meeting for many a day to come. On the 17th the blow fell which we had so long anticipated.

4. ARRESTED !

On the 7th of September we had stated in the *Volksstaat* that we knew from the most reliable sources that the Saxon Government intended to take energetic proceedings against our party, at the instance of those at the German headquarters, Count von Bismarck in particular. Shortly afterwards the whole press, and the Liberal press more especially, began a regular hue and cry after us. They even had the insolence to accuse us of high treason, the supposed offence being committed in the interests of France. To make us further suspect, the papers published garbled extracts from our letters to the Party Committee, which had been seized when the members of the committee were arrested. Of course these extracts could only be published through the gross negligence or perjury of the official who had these letters in his keeping.

On the 17th of December I was at work in my workshop when my wife, pale as death, suddenly rushed in and informed me that a police official wished to speak to me. I knew at once what was the matter. The officer told me that he was to arrest me and seize my papers. The latter duty was soon accomplished, as I had destroyed most of them. I dressed rapidly and took leave of wife and child, assuring them that I should soon be back. A cab took us to the police-station and thence to the prison. I was put into a cell, and I will not conceal the fact that when the door was locked and bolted I ran furiously to and fro and cursed my enemies. The next morning—it was a Sunday—the Public Prosecutor and the Director of the prison came to see me and asked me whether I had any requests to make. I asked for books and a light up to 10 p.m. The director granted this request, except that I could not have a light later than 8 p.m. The Public Prosecutor informed me that my entire career as an agitator would be investigated, as it was regarded as dangerous to the State and treasonable. The investigation would take a long time, as it was intended that evidence should be obtained from abroad. On the following day I was to make my first appearance before the examining judge. I was on tenterhooks. The judge, Ahnert, received me with a serious demeanour and was very reserved. He told me that we should be tried—for I learned that Liebknecht and our sub-editor, Hepner, had been arrested also—on a charge of attempted high treason. I was greatly surprised and disappointed when the judge told me that he could not for the present continue my examination, as the principal documents which constituted the material for the prosecution were still in Brunswick. However, he hoped to receive them before the end of the year. Thus we had, strictly speaking, been arrested illegally, as neither judge nor Public Prosecutor was acquainted with the material of the indictment. Evidently those at headquarters had been anxious to render us innocuous as promptly as possible.

I was extremely wroth when I returned to my cell. I now had ample leisure to inspect my lodging. It was roomy enough, being almost empty. In one corner was a great covered wooden tub, intended for purposes on which I need not enlarge. On one wall was a small shelf, with a water-jug, a hymn-book, and the New Testament. On the other side of the cell, also fixed against the wall, was a narrow bench, three feet in length, and in front of it stood a very small table (this was a special favour), so small that an open copy of the *Gartenlaube* * entirely covered it. There was no bed ; a mattress was spread on the floor for the night, and removed in the morning. From below my window, which was, of course, cross-barred, and so high up in the wall that I could only reach it by standing on the table, a curious noise rose day and night. When I looked out I saw in a garden below six large coffee-roasters at work, roasting coffee for our troops at war in France.

My cell was abnormally cold, and the winter was very severe. The old-fashioned iron stove did not give out much heat ; it was started at five o'clock

A popular family magazine about the size of *Punch*.

in the morning with a few handfuls of coal. I had to get a little fresh air ; but if I opened the window the little warmth there was in the cell flew out. To keep myself warm I used to sit on the table, put my feet on the bench, and wrap my legs in a blanket which was given me, notwithstanding which I contracted inflammation of the bladder. Liebknecht, as our senior, had been given a better cell. I learned this from my wife, who was allowed to visit me once a week in the presence of the judge, and with whom I was allowed to correspond, again under the supervision of the judge.

I very soon discovered, to my great disgust, that my cell was infested with vermin, but by dint of much labour I succeeded in clearing them out. Hardly had I done so when, by order of the doctor, I was given a warmer cell on the west side of the prison, formerly occupied by a woman charged with infanticide, as the warder amiably informed me. The result of this move was that I had to do the work of cleansing all over again.

Imprisonment without or pending trial, such as ours was, is of all forms of imprisonment the most abominable. To be condemned to strict solitary confinement, behind bolt and bar, without knowing how long it is to last, or what the indictment will be, is exceptionally harassing and debilitating. At last, in the beginning of January, I was again brought before the judge. When I entered the room I saw on the window-sill a large bundle of blue paper—my letters to the Party Committee, which the secretary had most carefully kept, in spite of my warning. I don't know what I would have done to him if I had had him then and there under my thumb. But I soon found I had no cause to be angry. The judge told me he had received the papers only a few days earlier, but would inspect them as soon as possible. He was as good as his word. At every fresh examination he became more accessible. Of course he examined our letters first, and as most of these were strictly confidential, we had written, not only of party matters but of our personal troubles, great and small, so that the letters proved that we had not been lying on a bed of roses. To his surprise, I fancy, the judge discovered that we were not traitors and regicides, but just ordinary human beings actuated by the best of motives and with warm blood in our veins. By the end of February the judge had worked through the enormous mass of documents—some 2,000 letters—and closed the preliminary examination. The judge—a most intelligent and conscientious man, as we learned later from our counsel for the defence, Otto Freytag—had arrived at the conclusion that there was no case against us either for attempted high treason or actions preparatory thereto, and he therefore recommended our release. This the Public Prosecutor opposed.

Yet I was convinced that we should be condemned ; not that we were guilty, but on account of the hue and cry against us in the Press I had no confidence in the jury. Further, the Government, I was certain, being on its dignity, would do everything in its power to secure a verdict against us. I was prepared to receive two years in a fortress. And I was right.

There were to be new elections to the Reichstag on the 3rd of March. I was a candidate in my old constituency—Glauchau-Meerane in Saxony. Our party and the Lassalleans put me up as joint candidate at Leipzig, though I tried to dissuade them from doing so.

Our financial means were very small ; in no constituency was a larger sum spent than £25 to £30. The supporters of our party to-day can hardly conceive how little money we had to manage with.

The elections were unfavourable to us ; they proceeded to the accompaniment of the tolling of bells and the thunder of guns that celebrated the preliminaries of the Peace of Versailles. Only one other candidate of our party was elected beside myself ; the other four were defeated. In Saxony, we received altogether 39,000 votes ; the General Labour Union got altogether some 63,000 votes.

As soon as I received the news of my election I sent my constituents a letter from prison, thanking them warmly for their renewed confidence in me.

I have often experienced the pleasure of finding myself the object or subject of poetry, laudatory or otherwise. Thus, during the election, the following was circulated in my constituency :—

NAPOLEON UND BEBEL

Er sitzt auf Wilhelmshöhe,
Er im Bezirksgericht ;
Er hat sie in der Zehe,
Und er im Kopf die Gicht.

"One of them sits on Wilhelmshoh',
One on a prison bed ;
The one has gout in his big toe,
The other in his head."

At Leipzig the lampoons appeared even during our imprisonment. At a music-hall a farce was presented entitled " Nebel and Piepknecht " ; at another, " Bebel : or the enlightened Cobbler and his Boy." In this way the " patriots " sought to give vent to their anger against us.

Part of the Liberal Press was so incensed at my re-election that it did everything in its power to prevent my release from prison for the Session of the Reichstag. But the Saxon Government, in order to prevent any discussion, released us on the 28th of March. At four in the afternoon the warder suddenly entered my cell with the news that we were to be released. Leaving the cell, I found Liebknecht and Hepner in the corridor. Without speaking a word we embraced one another. The examining judge before whom we were brought informed us of our release, but we had to promise not to leave the Leipzig district without his permission.

Two days later the Brunswick Committee was also released. The High Court had refused to prosecute it for high treason. The committee had been 200 days in prison, we 101 days. The members of the committee were later condemned, merely for various transgressions of the laws of association, to terms of fourteen and sixteen months' imprisonment, but on appeal the terms were reduced to two and three months.

NOTE.—Members of the Reichstag may be released from prison if not yet condemned, as was the case with Bebel. Generally, the Reichstag passes a motion to postpone trial until after the Session closes. If the Reichstag does not pass a motion—as was the case with Bebel in later years—prisoners are generally not released.

CHAPTER XV

FURTHER PARLIAMENTARY ACTIVITY. THE TRIAL FOR HIGH TREASON

1. THE FIRST SESSION OF THE GERMAN REICHSTAG.

ON the 2nd of April I went to Berlin to attend the sittings of the Reichstag, which had been opened with due solemnity by the Emperor in the presence of all the German princes and representatives of the Free Towns.*

First of all, I went to my former landlady to inquire whether she could put me up again. To her great regret she had to refuse, informing me that in the previous December, when we had left Berlin, the police had come to her house and had strongly objected to her taking us in. We had been under the surveillance of the secret police during the whole Session, just as though we had been criminals.

---

* Three of the old Hanse Towns—Hamburg, Bremen, and Lübeck—which enjoy a sort of republican Constitution.

In the Reichstag, as there was no room on the Left, I had to take my seat on the extreme Right. The neighbourhood of the honourable members of the Right was by no means welcome to me, but I must confess they behaved as gentlemen, and did not make me pay for my misfortune.

The debate on the first reading of the Constitution of the Empire, which was presented for ratification, was monopolised by the *Kultur-Kampf* speeches.* The declaration of the dogma of papal infallibility by the Council of the Vatican in Rome (1870) had stirred up the Opposition. The Liberals evinced a burning desire to disguise their shame at having sacrificed their ideals of civic liberty by floods of high-sounding oratory about the *Kultur-Kampf*—a term invented by Professor Virchow.† The Catholic party had become the Centre, under the leadership of Windthorst.‡ I delivered a speech expressing my astonishment at the religious turn which the debates had assumed. For one who, like myself, I added,

* The struggle, headed by Bismarck, against the Roman Catholic Church in Germany was known as the *Kultur-Kampf* (lit. "War of Culture").

† The famous Berlin scientist-professor of pathology—a lifelong Radical, and a most consistent and implacable opponent of Bismarck's policy.

‡ A former Minister of the ex-King of Hanover (who was deposed in 1866), another implacable enemy of Bismarck's.

had long ago broken with all religious dogmas, it cost not a little self-sacrifice to continue attendance. I finished my speech by expressing a hope —this amid general uproar—that before the end of the nineteenth century the demands of the Social-Democratic party would be realised. Time has seemed to show that this expectation was rather too optimistic.

I also had an encounter with Miquel. But when I alluded to the fact that he had once belonged to the party he now attacked, namely, the Communists, the House was nonplussed, and Miquel remained silent. From that time onward Deputy Miquel treated me with something like respect.

The Radicals again brought forward a motion recommending the payment of Members. I taunted our opponents with the dread of the Social-Democrats, which set them against it. Bismarck frankly treated the motion as a farce. Many of the Members then present, he said, would certainly never be returned if the payment of Members were introduced ! And that would be a pity, for he nourished in his heart a certain tenderness for the present assembly. Yet, he must add, the Prussian Upper Chamber, which was not paid, was inclined to curtail its Sessions, while the Lower Chamber, which was paid, showed an opposite tendency !

When a motion was before the House for more

money to bring the war to an end, I again explained
our standpoint. No French Government, whatever
its nature, would be allowed to forget the annexation of Alsace-Lorraine. France would look
for allies, and would try Russia. Germany would
have to maintain a much greater army. At the
end of my speech I praised the Commune—it had
been proclaimed on the 18th of March—for its
moderation. I did not sympathise with all the
Commune had done, but we in Germany, in a
similar situation, should certainly not observe the
same moderation towards the great financiers.

As I stood quite alone in the Reichstag—my
colleague did not count—I had to be more
frequently in Berlin. Yet my business urgently
required my presence in Leipzig. Those who were
jubilant over my doings in the Reichstag had no
idea how miserable I sometimes felt!

On the 25th of May I was once more in the
thick of the battle. I spoke against the coercion
of Alsace-Lorraine. At the close of my speech I
took the opportunity of defending the Commune.
The European proletariat, I explained, looked
hopefully towards Paris. The fighting in Paris
was only a mere skirmish of outposts, and before
many years had gone the battle-cry of the French
proletariat, " War upon the palaces, peace to the
cottages, death to misery and idleness ! " would

be the battle-cry of the whole European proletariat. Then the time would come when the
proletariat would have won the right of self-
government, which could only be realised under
a Republican form of government. Prince
Bismarck said in the autumn of 1878, when
he introduced his anti-Socialist laws, that it was
this speech of mine which had opened his eyes
to the dangers of Socialism. If that was so, he
showed no signs of the fact at the time. He simply
brushed my speech aside as not worthy of a reply ;
the other speakers did the same, but the Press
attacked me all the more violently, although the
Berliner Börsen Zeitung brought out a Sunday
feuilleton, written probably by Stettenheim, then
editor of *Wasps*, a satirical weekly, which poked
fun at the alarm of the bourgeois, and sought to
show that, after all, I was not such a very
dangerous incendiary.

At this time I made the acquaintance of Johann
Most. As a Socialist, and for his participation in
the Eisenach Congress, he had been condemned
in Austria to a term of penal servitude for high
treason, but was released by a general amnesty,
expelled from Austria, and came to Leipzig. In
a letter to his father, who urged him to abandon
his errors, he said he would rather receive dry
bread from his party than one thousand gulden a

month from the bourgeois parties. This says much for his character ; and it was his honest opinion, for he was at heart a man of sterling character. If, later on, under the anti-Socialist laws, he went astray and became an anarchist and an advocate of direct action, and finally, atlhough he had been a model of abstinence, ended in the United States as a drunkard, it was all due to the anti-Socialist laws, laws which drove him and many others from the country. Had he remained under the influence of the men who were able to guide him and restrain his passionate temper, the party would have possessed in him a most zealous, self-sacrificing, and indefatigable fighter. In later years he attacked me most violently in his paper, *Freiheit*, which he edited from London, and later from New York ; yet I am heartily sorry that one who had such valuable gifts should have perished so miserably.

The party soon recovered from the effects of the war. The great industrial prosperity that ensued favoured the movement. That the " German question " had been solved, though not as we had wished, yet definitely for the present, removed many points of difference that had kept the Labour party divided. The field of battle became simplified and easier to overlook. Our party, the Eisenacher as we were now called, soon had a number of papers in different towns, in which our ideas were propagated.

2. THE DRESDEN CONGRESS. THE SECOND SESSION OF THE REICHSTAG.

The second party Congress was held in Dresden, on the 12th, 13th, and 14th of August, 1871 ; 56 delegates attended, representing 75 localities and a membership of 6,220. I was president. The agenda was interesting and the debates lively. In place of Liebknecht, who was unable to attend, Most had to report upon the political standpoint to be adopted by Social-Democracy. The debates gave rise to violent scenes. The inspector of police who was present demanded in the name of his superiors that no allusions must be made to the Paris Commune. We refused, and the report of Most was all the more combative. I proposed, as it was unworthy of us to debate under such conditions, that the resolution should be passed without debate, adding that " after the publication of the official documents relating to the Commune it was evident that the statements against the Commune, which had been made for months, were calumnious lies." The resolution expressly approved of the attitude of the *Volksstaat*—that is, our attitude towards the events of the preceding year, including, of course, the war—and especially of the bonds of intellectual unity between German Social-Democracy and the " International," which were promoted by our journal. Finally, we decided to express our gratitude to the Paris Commune without debate, by rising from our seats.

Hamburg became the headquarters of the Party Committee, and Berlin of the Committee of Control. The Congress was to be held the following year at Mayence.

Shortly after the Dresden Congress the first women's meetings were held in Leipzig and Chemnitz, and in the latter town the first Women's Union was founded.

In the Reichstag, during the Session of 1871, I spoke against the Budget. I warned the Liberals that the hopes of a diminished budget, now that the Empire had been established, were a delusion. The increasing hostility of class to class would alone prevent any decrease. Yet the standing army would not always under all circumstances remain the support of the existing order of things. France had possessed a large army, yet that army could not prevent the Commune. The proletariat increases more rapidly than any army can be increased ; and as an army increases, its Social-Democratic elements also increase, all the more rapidly as the industrial proletariat furnishes an ever larger proportion.

In another debate I came into violent collision with the President, Simpson. A Liberal motion demanding elected assemblies in all the Federated States was before the House, and I supported the Conservatives and the Centre in this matter, who opposed the motion, disregarding the sneers at the alliance of " red " with " black." *
I spoke against the motion as a delusion and a snare, and characterised the Constitution of the Empire as a piece of sham constitutionalism and naked Cæsarism. The President became more and more restive, and threatened to appeal to the House as to whether I should be heard any farther. I protested against this threat as illegal and against the rules of the Reichstag ; but, as I continued, the President put the question and obtained a majority.

Next day I protested that the House had broken its own rules. A Member could be suspended only after two calls to order, and the President had never formally called me to order. Finally, the President consented to submit the question to the Standing Committee on Procedure.

The matter caused great excitement outside the Reichstag, and most of the papers stood by me, claiming the right of free speech. The committee

* The centre is nicknamed " black " on account of its clerical tendencies,

very cleverly avoided the direct issue, and merely reported that it was not considered necessary for the President to use the express form of words, " I call you to order." I refused to accept this decision. On the motion of that old diplomatist Windthorst, the decision was referred back again to the committee. The President, regarding this procedure as a vote of no confidence, resigned, but was, of course, re-elected. Some of the Liberals were greatly incensed at the spectacle of barefaced vacillation which the Reichstag had afforded, and one of them, Ziegler, as soon as the resolution was passed, came over to my seat, trembling with anger, and said : " You are right, Bebel, we are no better than a pack of rascals ; you ought to hang the lot of us ! " I replied, laughingly, that if circumstances permitted I would not fail to follow his amiable advice.

My general attitude during the three last sessions had gained me considerable popularity among the working-classes and the democratic bourgeois circles, for genuine democracy still survived in certain sections of the middle classes. In Berlin, for example, there was a group of well-to-do citizens who followed the lead of Johann Jacoby. These— they were known as the Jakobites—had their own journal, a democratic weekly, *Zukunft*, which they maintained at a great loss, wealthy though they were, from 1867 to 1871. The editor-in-chief was Dr. Guido Weiss. To this group belonged William Spindler,* the son of the founder of the great clean-ing and dyeing firm ; van der Leeden, Dr. G. Friedländer, Morten Levy, Dr. Meierstein, Boas, Dr. Stephani, late editor of the *Vossische Zeitung,* and others.† When Liebknecht and I stayed over the week-end in Berlin we usually met these people in a wine-shop. Sometimes we were joined by Paul Singer. By tacit agree-ment we all drank the same cheap Moselle— the so-called *Kutscher* (coachman) at sixpence the tumbler. We would often go on to some beer-house ; I was a very poor hand at drinking, but some of the others could carry a good cargo. More than once we went home after sunrise.

Another consequence of my popularity was that the families of my friends made much of me, and invited me to dinners and suppers. I did not care much for these invitations, and avoided them as much as possible, as I used to be anxious to get home to my wife and family.

The *Allgemeine Zeitung* of Augsburg wrote : " Bebel again gave proof of brilliant oratorical

* Spindler learned his trade in England, and was the first dry-cleaner and dyer in Germany.

† It is curious to note that these genuine democrats are, to judge by their names, mostly Jews or non-Germans.

gifts, and of the fact that he is indeed a man. It is worth stating, especially as it is too little known, that this young master-turner of Leipzig, although he stands quite alone, and although his extreme views are generally condemned and regretted, has made for himself quite an exceptional position in the Reichstag, and has won the respect and recognition of the majority of the Members, and especially of the High Tories, the more so because, in the hours he can spare from his parliamentary labours, he works in the shop of a fellow-craftsman for the support of his family."

The latter statement was of course a fairy-tale. Such a thing would have been quite impossible. But I found this legend repeated later on in a book on Social-Democracy. It stuck ; thus history is made.

In the meantime the development of the party was quite satisfactory. It grew by the very persecution and opposition it encountered. In the meetings I had to fight, not only our ordinary adversaries but, as a rule, a host of speakers and agitators of the General German Labour Union. Although Schweitzer had resigned, the attacks upon us were even more violent than before under the new president, Hasenclever. After one meeting, at which we had been subjected to the most violent attacks, I took some of the speakers aside and reproached them with their treacherous tactics. They replied almost immediately that they had to attack us, for if Social-Democracy were to unite the next thing would be that the Government would proceed against the party and suppress it. Subsequent happenings have shown that this was an intelligent anticipation of coming events.

In the meantime a good many Social-Democrats had gone to prison. On the 1st of February, 1872, Valteich was interned in the fortress of Hubertus-berg ; Karl Hirsch followed him a little later.

3. The Trial for High Treason at Leipzig.

At the opening of the Reichstag on the 23rd of March, 1871, Prince Bismarck went up to Deputy Von Schwarze * and asked him : "Well, Herr Attorney-General, what will become of the prosecu-tion of Bebel and company? "

" Nothing at all," replied Von Schwarze, shrugging his shoulders.

" In that case," replied Bismarck, " these people ought not to have been imprisoned ; now, of course, the odium of the prosecution will fall upon us."

Schwarze, who had studied all the documents, meant to imply that he did not think a condemna-tion possible. Bismarck seemed to have forgotten that we were imprisoned—at his own instigation, so I was told—not on suspicion of high treason,

* The highest judicial functionary of Saxony.

but just to put us out of the way, behind prison doors.

* Our trial was to take place in the spring of 1872, at the Leipzig Assizes. As the excitement was considerable, we admonished our friends, by means of a manifesto in the *Volksstaat*, to keep quiet and not to play into the hands of the police and the *agents-provocateurs*. The Leipzig bourgeois papers thought it their first and most important duty to prejudice the jury against us by inflammatory articles which were expressly sent to members of the jury, and the latter were even approached personally in various ways.

I cannot attempt here to give a complete account of the trial, which lasted fourteen days. The indictment was based upon our whole activity as agitators as exemplified by our relations with the workers' societies, our behaviour at meetings, and our writings, whether in the form of newspaper articles, pamphlets, or letters, &c. Moreover, the entire mass of Social-Democratic pamphleteering literature which had so far appeared in German was used against us, whether we had any hand in its production or distribution or not.

The president of the court was a Herr von Mücke, who, in contrast with his name (Mücke =

* Bebel, it will be remembered, had been released from prison to attend the sittings of the Reichstag.

gnat), was a man of Herculean proportions, but with a brow so low that there seemed to be no room for brains. He was, as a matter of fact, a man of rather low intelligence. He had not mastered the rather voluminous indictment, and Socialism was a sealed book to him. He did not understand our explanations, and made himself ridiculous by his cross-examinations.

Otto and Bernhard Freytag were our counsels. They did very well, and more than once confounded the president by their cross-examination.

The jury comprised six tradesmen, one aristo-cratic landowner, one head forester, and a few small landowners. The court was crowded every day. The Minister of Justice and the Attorney-General were present on several occasions. As the leading papers of Germany gave extensive reports of the trial, their readers became for the first time aware of what Socialism meant and at what it aimed. The trial thus became eminently serviceable from the propagandist point of view; and we, especially Liebknecht, who was the chief protagonist, were not loath to avail ourselves of this opportunity. But our opponents, day after day, were hard at work seeking to prejudice the jury against us, meeting them in the restaurant, when the events of the day were discussed and exploiting these to our disadvantage.

On the thirteenth day the "pleadings" for and against us commenced. The Public Prosecutor closed his speech with the words: "If you do not find against the accused, you will sanction high treason for all time to come."

Our counsel replied, and tore the indictment to tatters ; but after two and a half hours of deliberation the jury came in with a verdict of guilty. The Public Prosecutor demanded two years' imprisonment in a fortress, and the court passed judgment accordingly.

Our party friends were exceedingly angry on hearing the verdict and sentence ; but I, feeling reckless, proposed that we should go all together to Auerbach's cellar—rendered famous by the scene in Goethe's *Faust*—and have a bottle of wine. Our wives, who received us with tears, were not pleased with our levity ; but finally, plucky women that they were, they came with us. My doctor consoled my wife in a curious way. "Frau Bebel," he said, "if your husband gets a year in prison you may rejoice, for he needs a rest ! "

On the 27th of March, when we had received the written verdict, we issued a brief manifesto to the party, admonishing them to be true to the cause, and especially to assist in the distribution of the *Volksstaat*, which then had a circulation of 5,500 copies. On the same day we published a

declaration in the *Volksstaat* protesting our innocence of the crime for which we were condemned,
and accusing the jury of partiality. "This trial,"
we said, "has done so much to propagate our ideas
that we willingly take a few years in prison as
part of the bargain. Social-Democracy is beyond
the reach of any jury. Our party will live, grow,
and conquer. But you, gentlemen of the jury, by
your verdict, have passed sentence of death on the
present system of trial by jury, for the jury composed of members of the propertied classes is
nothing but an instrument of class domination and
class oppression."

The entire democratic and radical Press was
on our side. The President and the Public Prosecutor were decorated for their "State-saving"
action. And on the 2nd of April Johann Jacoby
declared his secession from the bourgeois to the
Social-Democratic Labour party. Numerous protests were made by our party Press and at
public meetings, which gave rise to further
prosecutions.

Shortly after the trial I fell dangerously ill with
pleurisy. I was thoroughly exhausted with all this
work and worry, public and private. I suffered
violent pain, and could not sleep. During the
nights, as I lay awake, I bethought myself of Bismarck, in the light of a fellow-sufferer ; for I knew

from the papers that he was very ill with insomnia and neuralgia. "Grief is half removed when it is shared."

4. Further Speeches in the Reichstag and Trial for "Lèse-Majesté."

At the end of April, 1872, the Reichstag met for its third Session. Just restored to health, I proceeded to Berlin, and on the 1st of May spoke in support of the motion in favour of the abolition of the salt-tax. I opposed all taxes on the necessaries of life because the propertied classes maintained this system of taxation from purely selfish motives of class interest, so as to shift the public burdens from their own shoulders. Such a condition of affairs, I said, would certainly do nothing to reconcile the different classes of society.

The year 1872 saw the culminating phases of the *Kultur-kampf*, that greatest of Bismarck's political blunders, which gave the internal development of Germany a most pernicious tendency. The Bill before the Chamber was Bismarck's measure for the expulsion of the Jesuits. I spoke opposing it in the debate on the third reading, stigmatising it as a measure of coercion, which would only result in increasing the influence of the Jesuits in Germany, while the best means of combating that influence would be to spend the hundreds of millions then wasted on armaments on the education of the people.

The points of my speech were briefly as follows: The English historian Buckle measures the stage of development to which a people has attained by the degree of importance assumed by religious strife in the affairs of that nation. Measured by that standard Germany stands on a very low level of civilisation. The religious question holds the centre of the stage. Yet it must be admitted that religious questions are intimately allied to political and social problems. If the Centre party is strong in the House, that is not solely on account of its religious opinions, but especially on account of the social and political interests it represents. Those strata of the German people which profess the Roman Catholic faith and are economically retrograde adhere by preference to the Centre, while the other capitalistic strata join the Liberals. Protestantism, a plain, simple, homely religion—so to speak, a religion in dressing-gown and slippers—is the religion of the modern bourgeoisie. The whole battle, as far as religion is concerned, is a sham fight; in reality the fight is for the predominant position in the State. If the Liberals are in earnest in their professions of progress, they ought to break with the Church; for in reality the bourgeoisie has no religion at

all. Religion with them is only a means to an end ;
the end being the maintenance of authority, designed to make the workers more willing objects
of exploitation.

The dogma of infallibility is said to be a
danger to the State. That is a proposition I
cannot understand. In the end all dogmas are
antagonistic to science and reason, and are on that
account a danger to the State. But the more
monstrous a dogma—and the dogma of Papal infallibility certainly deserves to be called monstrous
—the more will it be resisted by all thinking people.
Again, Jesuitism was said to be immoral ; yet
the State as such had never cared a tinker's curse
for morality, and the then Chancellor was the
last man to do so. If the Jesuits and the
Centre would only support his policy, they would
be allowed to do as they liked in religious matters.
Bismarck wanted the Ultramontane party to become
an instrument of his policy. To oppose Jesuitism
by an emergency measure would only serve
to increase the number of its adherents. It
is indeed the State that is the real parent of
Jesuitism. Instead of spending hundreds of
millions yearly on instruments of murder, it
should spend these sums on the education of the
people. This would damage Jesuitism more than
all the coercion Acts in the world. To create a

really modern system of education, to separate the State from the Church, to expel the Church from the schools would in ten years put an end to all ecclesiastical intrigues. Let them preach in the Churches to their hearts' content—nobody will go to hear them. But the other parties do not want this. They want the help of authority, which is also the main support of the Church. If authority were to fail in heaven, it would drag down earthly authority with it. This would mean, as a political result, a Republican Government, the social system known as Socialism, and the religion of Atheism.

Count Ballestrem, the Centre deputy, fastened on my last remarks. "If the people," he said, "once lost their faith in a heavenly paradise, they would ask for the paradise on earth promised by the International." To which I replied with an emphatic "Quite right, too !"

An amusing incident was related among the deputies about this time. Some deputies of the Centre, chatting in a restaurant, were speaking of Döllinger, and his opposition of the dogma of infallibility. A clerical gentleman, deputy for Munich, was reported to have said : "Why, if the old ass believed in so much nonsense already he could surely have believed in this dogma as well !"

I was put on my trial for *lèse-majesté* because

I had criticised the King of Prussia's rescript of thanks, dated the 25th of June, 1870. The King had stated in this rescript that he trusted that freedom and unity would result from the war. I said we had got unity, but liberty was absent. It was the old story once more ; when kings were embarrassed they made all sorts of fine promises, but when the people, by its sacrifices, had saved them, they forgot all about their promises. I conducted my own defence. The Public Prosecutor asked for further imprisonment in a fortress, in addition to that to which I had already been condemned ; but the court overruled him, and condemned me to nine months in prison. The court also declared my mandate to the Reichstag annulled. This was a gross political blunder ; for as the law could not declare me ineligible I was again supported as candidate by my party, and triumphantly returned. This was a smack in the face for the court, but of this more anon.

CHAPTER XVI

IN THE FORTRESS! AND THE MEANTIME

1. HUBERTUSBURG.

BEFORE I set out for the fortress a friend wrote, in a farewell letter: "If it were not for your families, I could almost shout for joy over the stupidity of your enemies. You, for example, will certainly profit largely in health and will learn much ; then you will be a dangerous fellow indeed, and your good wife, in spite of the pangs of separation, will be content if you undergo a cure which will strengthen you for good."

On the first day of my imprisonment I published a declaration to my constituents, asking them to return me at the top of the poll, so as to set at naught the decision of the court, which they did. For when the Reichstag was to meet again, in the first months of 1873, the Saxon Government had to order a new election in my constituency, and I was returned by a majority four thousand votes larger than at the previous election.

I made an unsuccessful application to the Saxon Government to be released from the fortress in order to attend the sessions, it being maintained that the immunity of deputies guaranteed by Article 41 of the Constitution did not extend to prisoners. Although I think that in a constitutional State a deputy when in prison ought immediately to be released when he is required to attend to his duties in Parliament, I did not regret the refusal. A temporary release would have extended my imprisonment over a longer period and would still further have damaged my business affairs.

On the afternoon of the 8th of July I started on my journey to Hubertusburg. A crowd of both sexes was at the station to bid me goodbye. Amidst my luggage was a large cage with a cock canary, the gift of a Dresden friend, " as a companion in the prison cell." I got him a wife, and a goodly number of children and grandchildren were hatched to him in prison.

In Hubertusburg I found Liebknecht already installed. There was also Karl Hirsch and a party friend from Chemnitz. There were five or six of us altogether, and when one left the court would provide a fresh recruit. Further, there was always some student sent to the fortress for some duelling affair.

The Castle of Hubertusburg is quite a considerable pile of buildings in the baroque style. Our cells had large iron-barred windows, which overlooked the great kitchen garden, where we took our regulation walks, and beyond the walls over forest and field to the little town of Mutzchen.

The cleaning of our cells was done by a so-called " calefactor." We had to pay for this cleaning and rent as well—for the State does not give prison-room even for nothing—at the rate of some fifteen shillings monthly. We got our food from an inn in a village near by. Our daily routine was as follows : We had to be ready dressed by seven o'clock, when the cells were opened for cleaning. In the meantime we had breakfast in the large corridor. Our friend Hirsch used to take this opportunity to play chess with another civilian prisoner, with whom he used to be continually quarrelling over the game. From eight to ten we were locked in our cells ; then we took our regulation walks in the garden. From twelve to three in winter and four in summer we were once more locked up, and then took our second walk, to be locked up at five or six, according to the season, until the cells were unlocked next morning. We had the right to burn a light until 10 p.m., and these hours I devoted to study. After some months I obtained permission to have Liebknecht locked up

with me in my cell, from 8 to 10 a.m., that he
might give me lessons in English and French. Of
course, we used to discuss our party affairs, and
I answered the business letters which my wife sent
me every day.

Liebknecht and I were great lovers of tea ; but
we could not get any, and we were forbidden to
make it ourselves on account of the danger from
fire. However, rules are made to be broken, and
I managed to smuggle in a spirit lamp and kettle
and the necessary ingredients. As soon as we were
locked up for the night I began to brew my tea ;
and in order to give Liebknecht the pleasure of
indulging in his favourite beverage, I had cut a
pole in the garden, which was about nine feet long,
to the end of which I attached a net of my own
making. As soon as tea was ready I knocked on
the wall—Liebknecht's cell was next to mine—and
I placed a glass of tea in the net ; I then thrust
the pole out of the window and swung the glass
round to Liebknecht's. In the same way we
exchanged newspapers.

As soon as I was fairly settled in my cell I completely broke down. Only the excitement and
labours of the last years had made me oblivious
of the utter state of exhaustion to which I was
reduced. Now, when the tension was relaxed and
I had to keep quiet, I broke down. But absolute

rest and fresh air soon put me on my feet again. So the doctor was quite correct when he told my wife that a year's fortress would be the best cure for me. When undergoing a medical examination subsequently it was even discovered that my left lung, in which tuberculosis had eaten a large hole, had healed during my internment. I was lucky again; what might have proved an injury did me good.

As I was now finally to be imprisoned for thirty-one months I resolved to make a thorough use of this time by filling up, to some extent, the gaps in my education. I studied history and political economy principally. I read Marx's "Capital" for the second time; only the first volume was then published; Engel's "Condition of the Working Classes in England"; Lassalle's "System of Acquired Rights"; Mill's "Political Economy"; the works of Dühring and Carey; Lavelaye's "Primitive Property"; Stein's "History of Socialism and Communism in France"; Plato's "Republic"; Aristotle's "Politics"; Machiavelli's "Prince"; Sir Thomas More's "Utopia"; von Thünen's "The Isolated State"; and others. Of the historical works which I then read I was most captivated by Buckle's "History of Civilisation" and Wilhelm Zimmermann's "History of the German Peasants' War." The last book inspired

me to write a popular essay with the title " The
German Peasant's War," with special regard to the
chief social movements of the Middle Ages. It was
published in book form, but confiscated later on
under the anti-Socialist laws. I did not neglect
natural science. I read Darwin's " Origin of
Species " ;   Haeckel's   " Story   of   Creation " ;
Büchner's " Force and Matter " and " Man's
Position in Nature " ; Liebig's " Letters on
Chemistry " ; and part of my time I devoted to
reading the classics. I was seized by a veritable
passion for reading and learning.

I translated from the French Ives Guyot's and
Sigismond Lacroix's " Study of the Social Doctrines
of Christianity " ; a translation which is published
down to the present day under the title " The True
Nature of Christianity."   I wrote a criticism of
this work in the shape of a pamphlet, entitled
" Glosses to Ives Guyot and Sigismond Lacroix :
the True Nature of Christianity," with an Appendix
on the present and future position of women. This
pamphlet was, as far as I know, the first thing ever
to be written by a man of our party on the position
of women from the socialistic point of view.   I
was induced to write it by my study of the French
socialistic and communistic Utopias.

I also made my preparatory studies to the book
" Woman," which first appeared in 1879 under the

title "Woman in the Past, Present, and Future," which, though prohibited under the anti-Socialist laws, rapidly ran through eight editions. In 1910 the fiftieth and fifty-first editions were published.

Every three or four weeks our families came to see us. They stayed for three days and lodged in the village. They used to bring our children. They were allowed to stay with us in our cells from 9.30 a.m. to 7 p.m., and to accompany us on our regulation walks. This was an alleviation indeed.

I experienced a great need of bodily exercise, and the notion struck me that I would do some gardening. We could not get garden plots allotted to us, but were allowed to cultivate as much as we liked of the fallow land along the garden wall. We set to work with great energy. Liebknecht, who was just then writing his essay on the land question, regarded himself as an expert on agrarian matters, and assured us that this fallow land was one of the most fertile of soils. But when we began to dig we found nothing but stone. Liebknecht pulled a long face, but we all laughed. We then took to spreading manure—not a very nice job, and one which we should have refused with indignation had the authorities forced us to do it.

We sowed radishes and awaited the harvest.

They came up beautifully—at least, the leaves did —but there were no radishes. Every morning when we started to take our walk there would be a race to see who should pull up first a radish. But always in vain. There were no radishes ; and finally the warder told us the reason : we had manured the ground too well. The soil was too fat. We looked very foolish indeed.

On the 29th of October King John of Saxony died, and his son Albert became King. As an amnesty is the rule when a new ruler ascends the throne, our wives hoped for our release. But we had no such illusions. The new King would rather have released all the criminals in Saxony than one of us. And we preferred it so ; for the general elections to the Reichstag were approaching, and we counted on the spirit of exasperation which was abroad at the time, and which would have been spoiled by an amnesty.

I decided to use my enforced leisure and profit by my absence from the electoral campaign in writing a pamphlet for the use of candidates, under the title " The Parliamentary Activity of the Reichstag and the other Assemblies and Social Democracy from 1871 to 1873." In an appendix I collected those paragraphs useful to know for practical politicians of the electoral law, the electoral ordinances, the criminal code, the law as to associations, as well as hints on party propaganda. I had the satisfaction of learning from Eugen Richter himself that my pamphlet inspired him to write his well-known " Political A B C." Later on the other parties all followed my example.

The elections took place on the 10th of January, 1874. They were very satisfactory to our party. Six of our candidates were elected, and three candidates of the German Labour Union. The two sections of the Social Democrats thus had nine members in the Reichstag. Altogether they had received 351,670 votes ; the candidates of the General German Labour Union received 180,319, and ours 178,351. The total number of votes was larger by 236,000 than in 1871, or by 200 per cent.

Of course, this brilliant result greatly angered the bourgeois parties. In view of the fact that in spite of prosecutions and chicanery the party was steadily increasing, the idea of attacking it by exceptional legislation, which already existed in the mind of the Government, now gradually began to take shape.

2. KÖNIGSTEIN.

In the course of March we were officially informed that on the 1st of April, 1874, we should be removed to the fortress of Königstein.

But the removal was postponed, so that Liebknecht completed his term at Hubertusburg, depart-
ing for Leipzig on April the 15th. I myself set
out for Königstein, accompanied by an official in
plain clothes, on the 23rd of the same month.
When we took our leave of the director of the
prison and thanked him for his many civilities he
was visibly touched ; he shook hands with us and
recommended us to the keeping of the Almighty
as the best viaticum, from his point of view, he
could give us.

The 23rd of April was a beautiful spring day.
We climbed up to the fortress, and on the way
met the Governor, General von Leonhardi, to whom
I was introduced by my warder. We continued
on our way in his company, the General inquiring
how we had been treated at Hubertusburg, and
promising that I should fare no worse at Königstein. I was given a room in a part of the building
which had formerly served as a powder magazine,
with bomb-proof walls and iron-barred, portlike
windows. There was a big, tiled stove in the
room, which greedily devoured the 5 lbs. of coal
—the meagre daily allowance—without giving any
warmth to the room, in spite of the brilliant spring
weather. I had to buy extra coal at my own
expense in order to keep warm.

There was very little space for walks in the

confined quarters of the fortress ; a sentry mounted guard in order to keep the numerous visitors at a distance. But the food, which I got from the canteen, was both ample in quantity and excellent in quality.

3. ZWICKAU.

On the 14th of May I was released. Before serving my nine months in prison I was granted six weeks' leave. In Leipzig I was greeted by Eduard Bernstein, who had come from Berlin expressly for the purpose. It was Whitsuntide, and I made an excursion with my family and friends to the " Saxon Switzerland " ; and when we came to Königstein, which I had just left, we were highly amused by the fact that the window of the cell in which I had slept for three weeks was pointed out as one of the curiosities of the place.

Before entering on my term of imprisonment at Zwickau I called on the director to learn the privileges which would be allowed to a political prisoner. I was to be allowed to see my wife once a month, in the presence of a warder. But after the first visit, in the third month of my imprisonment, we resolved to forego further meetings ; for having to put up with an official witness to every word we uttered the interview was not worth the cost of the journey.

I was much troubled by business anxieties. The industrial crisis was then at its height, and it was only with great difficulty that my business could compete with that of a rival who had started production by machinery on a large scale.

My principal occupation was the writing of the history of the German Peasants' War—now long out of print—not a masterpiece at any time, as I lacked the necessary means of reference. I wrote the book because the wars of 1525 and the preceding peasant revolts seemed to me one of the most important phases of modern German history, and withal a period shamefully neglected by the official historians.

At last, on the 1st of April, 1875—Bismarck's sixtieth birthday—I was released. I had been on the best of terms with the prison authorities, and my parting from the director was most cordial. It has always been my way to make the best of things that cannot be mended. Without in the least demeaning myself, I have always tried to facilitate the difficult task of the prison authorities by conforming strictly to the regulations.

My comrades at Zwickau gave me an ovation on the day of my liberation, and presented my wife and myself with two fine coffee-cups with suitable inscriptions, and with the wish that we might enjoy the national beverage of Saxony in quiet and repose for ever thenceforth ; a wish, alas ! that was not to be granted.

My friend Sonnemann, the chief proprietor of the *Frankfurter Zeitung*, published a leader congratulating me on my release instead of Bismarck on his sixtieth birthday. He had sent me some bottles of wine while I was in prison, which I had sent home to drink with my wife and friends, as the prison regulations do not allow such luxuries.

Shortly after my release I received a letter from Professor Schäffle, the sociologist, formerly a member of the Liberal Government of Austria, and the author of the well-known pamphlet, " The Quintessence of Socialism," which had caused a great stir by its unprejudiced account of the aims of Socialism. He sent me the first volume of his *magnum opus*, " The Structure and Life of the Social Body." He wrote that although we might hold different opinions on many points, we were equally interested in social questions, and asked me to accept this book as a token of common interests.

Later, in 1877, we met in Leipzig. Our principal subject of conversation was the development of the Socialist party and the time when Socialism would be predominant. I, optimist that I am, thought the time close at hand ; he thought it would take at least two hundred years.

But Professor Schäffle underwent a complete transformation. When Bismarck inaugurated his social reforms, Schäffle, who was anxious to take office under him, wrote a pamphlet on the "Impracticability of Social Democracy," which was diametrically opposed to his former convictions. After this performance I had no further relations with him.

CHAPTER XVII

FROM 1871 TO THE GOTHA CONGRESS

1. GOVERNMENTS AND SOCIAL-DEMOCRACY.

THE Paris Commune made all the Governments of Europe regard the Socialist movement with the keenest anxiety. This anxiety increased when it became evident that the Commune had the sympathy of the workers of those countries in which a Socialist movement was already in being. Governmental and bourgeois circles nursed exaggerated, not to say ridiculous, ideas of the power of the "International." Many voices were raised in Germany demanding that the movement should receive a more vigorous handling, a demand very willingly conceded by the police and the courts.

Bismarck invited his most inveterate enemy, the Austrian Chancellor, von Beust, to confer with him with regard to the "International" at Gastein ; but they could come to no agreement further than to "study the question."

But in February, 1872, the Spanish Government

—Prince Amadeo of Italy having just been elected King of Spain—addressed a circular dispatch to the European Powers suggesting that one of the Great Powers should take the matter in hand and propose measures against the "International," which by its aims attacked the very traditions of humanity, wished to abolish the Deity, the family, and hereditary property, and by reason of its formidable organisation constituted a danger which could hardly be exaggerated. But the English Foreign Secretary, Lord Granville, extinguished the proposal. The "International," he declared, although a centre of an international union of workers and trades unions, restricted itself in Great Britain to giving advice in the event of strikes. It had very little money. By the laws of England any foreigner had the right to come to England and reside there, and enjoyed the protection of the laws of the land, on exactly the same footing as that of a British subject. They could only be punished if they transgressed these laws, and only by the regular courts and the ordinary public procedure. No foreigner as such could be expelled except subjects of countries with which treaties of extradition for criminal offences existed. So far he saw no reason for altering the laws respecting the sojourn of foreigners in Great Britain.

The attitude of the British Government made an

international agreement impossible ; and the Hague Congress of 1872, when the split occurred between the Socialists under Marx and the Anarchists under Bakunin, proved to such Governments as were over-timid that the danger was not immediate. Further, the " International," by transferring the locale of its General Council from London to New York, proved the need of reorganisation.

But Bismarck remained on the alert. In the Prussian Upper Chamber, in April, 1873, he spoke of the necessity of rigorous laws against the party of the " International " as well as against the party of ecclesiastical domination—the Centre. In June of the same year he brought in a Bill to limit the freedom of the Press to the effect that any one attacking, in print, the family, property, universal service, or any other of the fundamental supports of the existing order of things, in a manner detrimental to morality, the sense of justice, or patriotism, or representing actions punishable under this law as meritorious, consistent with duty, and worthy of imitation, or discussing the present condition of civil society in a manner likely to lead to a breach of the peace, should be punished by imprisonment or detention in a fortress for a term not exceeding two years. Offences against religion taking the form of attacks in the public Press were to be punishable by imprisonment for terms varying from three months to four years. The responsible editor was to receive the same punishment as the culprit.

These diabolical proposals were too much even for the majority in the Reichstag. The Bill was thrown out. Bismarck then tried to get at the Social-Democratic party by alterations of the laws of contract, the laws relating to master and man, and so forth. I shall speak of these attempts later. From 1874 onwards there was a continuous series of prosecutions which culminated, in the spring of 1878, after the attempts on the life of the Emperor William, in the anti-Socialist laws.

2. THE TWO SOCIAL-DEMOCRATIC PARTIES.

The character of the persecutions which the party suffered from 1872 onwards should have promoted a closer union, a more perfect co-operation of all socialistic bodies. But from 1872 to 1873 the internecine war raged more fiercely than ever, especially on the side of the Lassalleans—the General German Labour Union—whose especial bugbear was our chief agitator in Berlin.

The question of union was first mooted at the Congress of the Lassallean Union in Berlin in 1872 ; but the motion was defeated by putting the previous question. The matter was again discussed at the fourth Congress of the Social-Democratic Labour

Party, held in 1872 at Mayence. A lengthy resolution was adopted, recommending mutual forbearance, and especially the cessation of Press polemics. But although Liebknecht and I, in the *Volksstaat*, kept our promise and did not attack the other branches, made even proposals of a very conciliatory nature, recommending, if fusion were impossible, at least an agreement upon common action at elections, the quarrel continued with undiminished bitterness. We were even snubbed for our unauthorised attempts at reconciliation by the Committee of Control.

The director of the Leipzig police for the year 1873 was especially active in the persecution of our party, as if eager to outshine his colleagues throughout the country. Thus he published an edict prohibiting attendance at the Congress of the " International " at the Hague, under penalty of four months' imprisonment. Our co-editor Hepner contravened the edict, got his four months, and was afterwards expelled from Leipzig. Moreover, the director prohibited membership in the " International," forbade the recruiting of fresh members, and the collection of money for party purposes.

Hepner, owing to disagreements with the party executive, had written letters to Marx and Engel, in which he described the party as being in very low water, thanks to the Lassalleans. This, on account of the deep distrust which Marx and Engels felt for everything connected with Lassalle, caused the latter to write to Liebknecht in a spirit of admonition. The contents of this letter were communicated to me, and I wrote to Marx and Engels reassuring them. To Engels I wrote that as matters stood, it was impossible to take active measures against the Lassalleans without irreparably damaging the cause. The cult of Lassalle, as engineered by the Countess Hatzfeldt, must be uprooted. But we had to proceed carefully, as the posthumous influence of Lassalle was still immense. The best means of dealing the cult a decisive blow would be for Marx, as a recognised scientific authority on political economy, to expose, from a scientific and objective point of view, in a series of articles in the *Volksstaat,* the many faults and errors of Lassalle's theories. I wrote to Marx in the same strain, asking him also to publish a new edition of the " Communist Manifesto," omitting the conclusion, which as it stood would expose the publisher to prosecution for high treason. The Manifesto, strongly recommended and sold in public, would be an eye-opener to many, and would expose the weakness of Lassalle's proposals.

In those days the prosecutions against the *Volksstaat* were so numerous that usually two and sometimes three of its editors were in prison. The same fate befell the editors of the other party organs, which were eight or nine in number, not counting the *Volksstaat*. In Saxony the authorities not only imprisoned but expelled the offenders from town or district. The Leipzig police prohibited participation in the fifth Congress of the party at Eisenach—it was to have been held at Nürnberg, but the Bavarian Government prohibited it—under penalty of a month's imprisonment. Leipzig was therefore not represented at the Congress. It was attended by 71 delegates, representing 274 members. The question of the union of the two sections of the party was again discussed, but without any practical result, as the Labour Union had shortly before passed a resolution refusing in most abusive terms to have anything to do with the Social-Democratic Labour Party.

I have already mentioned the results of the elections of 1874. It may interest some to learn what these elections cost the party. The expenses borne by the party funds for the whole of Germany amounted to some £1,950 ; the Saxon party committee, for the 91,000 votes polled, spent some £112 ; the elections in Leipzig, borough and district, including a by-election, cost £109 ; at Chemnitz £65 was spent ; in other constituencies £22 and £52. These figures, compared with those of our own times, seem absurdly small. But now members of the party give money and are paid for election work. In those days they did not give money ; they had very little to give and they were few in number ; and they worked without pay. The individual member had to make much greater sacrifices than are usual now in order to obtain any results. Moreover, it must not be forgotten that to-day, in Germany especially, the election campaigns are conducted by our adversaries on a much more extensive and costly scale than any we had to contend with, so that we have to meet it by more strenuous exertions and a much greater expenditure.

3. THE SESSION OF 1874.

This Session commenced in February. Our proposal to the members of the General German Labour Union that we should unite our parliamentary fractions was declined ; but we had agreed that we would at least mutually support each other. Both sides had had enough of the mutual recriminations, which only profited our opponents, and were anxious for an understanding even though union might not be possible.

The party was not at all satisfied with its representatives in Parliament. (I was, of course, still in prison, and Liebknecht did not attend, as he was released only a short time before the adjournment.) It was urged that they spoke too rarely, and too mildly when they did speak. The brilliant result of the elections had raised expectations. Our members complained bitterly that the President of the Reichstag did not call upon them to speak, and showed a preference for the members of the General German Labour Union. This was quite true. Forckenbeck was then President, and he was, as I have already stated, one of the most partial Presidents the Reichstag had ever had. The prearranged list of speakers had been abolished in order to muzzle the Socialists. The members who wished to speak had to attract the attention of the President much as children bring themselves to the notice of their teacher. It was therefore left to his discretion to call upon whom he pleased, and Forckenbeck made ample and unblushing use of this discretionary power. Our members conse- quently very rarely had an opportunity of speak- ing. Another abuse of the rules of debate : there was a member of the National Liberal party, one Valentin, who was ever ready to move the closure ; so much so that a would-be speaker who was closured was said to be " Valentined "—that is, metaphorically, guillotined. Valentin was even said to keep motions for the closure in stock.

Among the Bills before the Reichstag was a new

Army Bill, which fixed the strength of the army on active service at 401,000 men for a term of seven years. The Liberals and National Liberals at first felt constitutional scruples, but the National Liberals finally gave in when Bismarck threatened to resign. It was then that Moltke uttered the oft-quoted words : " What we have gained by force of arms in half a year, that we must guard by force of arms for half a century ; for let us not deceive ourselves : we have won respect by our successful wars on all sides, but love on none."

To our proposals to transform the standing army into a militia Moltke replied : " Gentlemen, rifles are easily distributed, but not so easily taken back."

Another measure of importance to the working classes was an amendment of the industrial code penalising breaches of contract by fines not exceeding £7 10s. or imprisonment. The strikes which both during the boom and after the collapse had often been started without regard to contracts, had greatly alarmed the employers, who petitioned the Government and the Reichstag to make such breaches a criminal offence. The Government brought in the above measure, but the Reichstag threw it out ; it was not yet disposed to approve coercive legislation. It also rejected a Bill to restrain the freedom of the Press, although it was a somewhat milder measure than that cited in a former chapter.

The question of the union or fusion of the two wings of our party was again discussed at the Congress of 1874, but again without definite result. But what did not ensue as a result of friendly negotiations was finally achieved by persecution. It was more especially Tessendorf, who, as Public Prosecutor, was called from Magdeburg to the Berlin courts in 1873, who by his prosecutions acted as pacemaker ; and he was powerfully abetted in his efforts as a " saviour of the State " by the seventh chamber of the courts at Berlin, which in the numerous actions brought against members of our party proved itself a veritable " bloody assizes."

Tessendorf had already acquired fame in Magdeburg as a scotcher of Socialists. He was one of the worst of *Streber* (men on the make) in a time which produced such men in abundance. He wanted to make a career for himself, and sought to recommend himself to the ruling powers by his rigorous treatment of Socialism. He succeeded ; he eventually became Attorney-General of the highest court in Germany, the Imperial Court at Leipzig. But our party only grew stronger and more united as a result of his prosecutions. Those he set out to destroy were victors in the end. In the Berlin courts he justified the expectations of his superiors, and of Bismarck in particular. Prosecutions became more and more numerous ; penalties more and more harsh and brutal. Many a life was ruined, many a family's happiness destroyed. In most cases the offences tried were mere bagatelles, which any other court would have considered sufficiently punished by a few weeks of prison or a fine. Certain sections of society were in a state of "blue funk." In the whole of Prussia, during the year 1874, 82 Lassalleans were punished, in 104 trials, by a total of 212 months' imprisonment.

It was the same in Saxony. The judgments grew always more severe ; where formerly months were considered sufficient years were now inflicted. In Saxony it was our party that suffered the most.

In addition to these judicial proceedings the police persecuted us by dissolving our associations and in other ways. At the end of June the General German Labour Union was dissolved, and its president sentenced to two months' imprisonment. The police dissolved the Berlin branch of our party, the Union of Working Women and Girls, and the unions of bootmakers, cabinet-makers, and masons. The same thing happened in Frankfort, Hanover, and Königsberg. Saxony and Bavaria followed the example of Prussia.

All these prosecutions made it plain to the most

determined opponent of union that our only safety lay in a united front.

On the 11th of October, 1874, Liebknecht wrote me—I was in prison at Zwickau—to the effect that the Lassalleans had approached him with proposals of peace and fusion, but recommended caution. Later on it was agreed that our party executive at Hamburg should entrust a joint committee of the two sections with the task of considering conditions and plans of unification. Although there was opposition within the Labour Union, the subsequent negotiations pursued a favourable course. There was a mass meeting in Berlin, at which all the Reichstag deputies at liberty—two were in prison—spoke in favour of reunion. The committee, consisting of eight members of each section, met at Coburg, on the 14th and 15th of February, 1875, in order to arrive at a compromise between the two widely different programmes of the two sections of the party. The task was one of extreme difficulty, but finally the committee was able to announce that it had agreed upon a draft programme which satisfied all its members. But such was not the case with the party as a whole. When Liebknecht sent me the draft agreement in prison with the remark that it had not been possible to do more I was terribly upset. For weeks I had been in a state of suspense and ill-temper, because Liebknecht had not visited me as he had promised, nor had he thought fit to keep me *au courant* of the course of events. I thought a little more regard was due to me. I wrote a very long and very angry letter, in which I criticised the draft most severely, and worked out a long counter-proposal, going into the minutest detail. I thus proved once more that prolonged seclusion from the outside world causes one to become completely absorbed by one's own meditations. Liebknecht urged as excuse the pressure of work and the impossibility of speaking of intimate and secret party matters in the presence of prison officials. He was right ; but a prisoner who knows that negotiations are going on in the outside world which will affect the matters that completely absorb his thoughts and feelings, naturally longs for an interchange of ideas, be it ever so restricted. The party executive of course declined my proposals, and although I finally resigned myself I was never satisfied with the draft programme.

In a private letter to Engels I had asked for his opinion touching the matter of union. He answered in a decidedly negative sense. But I refrained from public criticism, under pressure from all sides and at Liebknecht's request ; my opposition, I was told, would make the union impossible. And as I had the union very much at heart, and the party was urgent in its demand for union, considerations of merely formal objection to the programme had to be put aside. After all, the programme could easily be amended later on.

After my release from prison—on April 1, 1875 —my constituency arranged to give me a grand reception at Glauchau, which I attended with my family. In a speech which I made on this occasion I alluded to the negotiations for union which were then in progress, and expressed the hope that as we had formerly fought each other we should now, with all our courage, strength, and endurance, wage war upon the common enemy.

CHAPTER XVIII

FROM THE CONGRESS OF UNIFICATION AT GOTHA TO THE EVE OF THE ANTI-SOCIALIST LAW

1. The Congress of Unification.

THE Congress of Unification was convened to meet at Gotha on the 25th of May, 1875. After years of bitter and mutual antagonism the hitherto hostile sections were to meet face to face and measure their forces. It is not surprising that they did not at once fall into one another's arms, but were still full of suspicion. Great mutual forbearance was required, for the differences of the two sections, personal and political, were still considerable. Our common enemies looked towards Gotha with breathless attention, anxious to learn whether the work of unification would be accomplished. It was accomplished, after a certain amount of friction, better than had been anticipated, and bore good fruit.

The Congress was attended by 127 delegates, representing 25,657 members; 71 delegates for

16,538 members of the General German Labour Union and 56 for 9,121 members of the Social-Democratic Labour party.

Liebknecht reported on the question of the programme. After some trifling amendments the following programme was unanimously adopted :—

1. Labour is the source of all wealth and all culture ; and as labour of a generally useful type is only made possible by society the whole product of labour is due to society, that is, to all its members, on condition that they recognise a general duty of labour, due by equal rights to each according to his rational needs.

In the present society the means of production are a monopoly of the capitalist class ; the resulting dependence of the working-classes is the cause of misery and servitude in all its forms.

In order that labour may be emancipated, the means of production must be transformed into the common property of society, and labour as a whole must be regulated on co-operative principles, and the product of labour applied to the commonweal in just division.

The emancipation of labour must be the work of the labouring classes, distinguished from which all other classes are but a mass of reactionary forces.

2. Starting from these principles, the Socialistic Labour Party of Germany aims by all legal means

at the establishment of a free commonwealth and a Socialistic society, the breaking of the iron law of wages by the abolition of the wages system, the extinction of every form of exploitation, and the removal of all social and political inequalities.

The Socialistic Labour Party of Germany, though working at first on a national scale, is conscious of the international character of the labour movement, and is resolved to assume all the duties which it imposes upon the workers in order to bring about in truth the fraternity of all human beings.

3. The Socialistic Labour Party of Germany, in order to pave the way for the solution of the social question, demands the institution of socialistic productive co-operation with State help under the democratic control of the people. These productive organisations, industrial and agricultural, are to be on such a scale that the socialistic organisation of the whole of labour shall result therefrom.

Then follow demands for the democratisation of the State and the immediate social demands.

The name of the unified party was to be the Socialistic Labour Party. As to organisation, it was to be directed by a board of five members, to be elected by the Congress. This directorate was to be supervised by a committee of control of seven members, to be elected by the members of the party in the city designated year by year as the headquarters of the committee by the Congress. A committee of eighteen members from all parts of Germany was to be elected, which was in the first instance to criticise the directorate and which would on occasions of importance be heard by the directorate. Local agents would be appointed by the directorate upon the proposal of local members.

In accordance with my motion Hamburg was selected as the first headquarters of the directorate. The following salaries were to be paid : to the president a monthly salary of some £9 15s., to his deputy £2 5s., to each of the two secretaries £7 10s., to the treasurer some £5 5s. monthly. The seat of the committee of control was Leipzig, and the president was myself. The official organs of the party were to be the *Neue Sozialdemokrat* in Berlin and the *Volksstaat* in Leipzig. Both were acquired by the party. The Congress separated with cheers for the workers of all civilised nations and the singing of the workers' Marseillaise.

In a letter to Engels I justified my acceptance of this programme. I agreed that the programme left much to be desired, and made too many concessions to the Lassalleans. Yet it was all that could be achieved at the time ; if we had asked for more we should have made the work of unification impossible, to the delight of our opponents and the detriment of the party. The rest would be a matter of education. My letter was not rightly understood. Engels complained that we had really been defeated by the Lassalleans and had accepted their meaningless phrases relating to State help, the iron law of wages, and so forth. He characterised our programme as confused, illogical, disconnected, and generally ridiculous in the highest degree.

It will be seen that it was not an easy matter to satisfy the two old gentlemen in London. What was really a clever tactical move on our part and the result of prudent calculation they regarded as mere weakness. However, the main point was achieved—and that was unification. It contained the germs of further development, and for that we could depend on our best friend the enemy.

2. AFTERMATH. MY ATTITUDE TOWARDS THE COMMUNE.

Of course all was not plain sailing even after the Congress of Unification. There was still dissension within the ranks, especially in Hamburg. In order to make the new unity a living reality it was agreed that the best-known men of the formerly divided camps should address meetings in those districts which had formerly been the reserves of the opposing sections. Thus Liebknecht made a tour of the north and west, some of the Lassalleans

took the south and Saxony, and I went to Hamburg
and Berlin, where I addressed large meetings.

For me personally the state of affairs was far
from agreeable. I suffered much from the antagonistic interests of public and private life. As I
had just taken a partner, the news spread through
Leipzig that I intended to retire from politics.
Thus a party friend wrote to me that he had been
told that I was about to start business on a large
scale, and gradually retire from the party. He
asked me to contradict these rumours publicly, a
course which I refused as being beneath my dignity.

The Autumn Session of the Reichstag in 1875
was the first I was able to attend after an absence
of nearly three and a half years. It was also the
first Session which we attended as a united party,
which made us altogether more energetic, active,
and independent.

A Bill was before the Reichstag to amend the
criminal law. Fourteen fresh offences were placed
in the category of criminal offences. Bismarck
was always a man of wrath, eager to crush and
abolish any tendency of the times which he
found inconvenient or disagreeable, by the application of coercive measures. He applied such
measures to the Roman Catholic Church, the Polish
nationalist movement, and to Social-Democracy.
And he was never converted from this standpoint,

although at the end of his life it was plain as the day that it had been a mistake. He was the vanquished, not the victor.

As the judges and the police had failed to suppress our movement, he now attempted to do so by amendments of the so-called political paragraphs of the criminal code. Thus paragraph 130 was to be worded as follows: "Whosoever, in a manner liable to cause a breach of the peace, shall publicly incite the different classes of the population one against the other, or in a similar manner shall attack by speech or writing the institutions of marriage, the family, or property, shall be punished by imprisonment." Other paragraphs were similarly amended. We decided, as a matter of tactics, to allow the Liberals to open an attack upon the amendments. Even the National Liberals declared against them. We took an active part in the debate on the amendment above quoted; the date was the 27th of January, 1876. The Minister of the Interior, Count Eulenburg, frankly admitted in the opening part of his speech: "Gentlemen, this paragraph is directed against Social-Democracy." The rest of his speech consisted of quotations from our newspapers, intended to prove that we were a menace to the State. He urged the Reichstag to pass the amendments, as otherwise, having regard to the

inadequacy of the law as it then stood, there was
a danger "that the rifles would go off and the
swords would pierce." His speech did not produce
the least impression, and Hasselmann, who spoke
for our party, had an easy task. Our party, he
declared, did not start the class war. It was commenced by our opponents, and the Paris Commune was there to prove how cruel and bloody was
their method of waging it. Finally he declared
that our party would continue the war by all legal
means. The end of the debate was that the Government could not find a single supporter for its Bill.
Our party Press warmly thanked Count Eulenburg
for his speech as a most excellent piece of propaganda, and it was decided that it should be printed
and distributed on the largest possible scale. Bismarck, too, did not fail to improve the occasion.
He complained that the Reichstag, when a Socialist
Deputy spoke, did not take him seriously. It was
necessary to contradict the Utopian nonsense of
the Socialists in the Reichstag, and give such contradiction the widest possible publicity. "Had not
the assassins and incendiaries of the Commune been
publicly praised in the Chamber, without a single
Deputy giving expression to the opposite view?
These phantom visions, which were revealed to
the infatuated only by the gloom of the dark lantern
of the seducers, ought to be dragged into the clear

light of the sun, in order to demonstrate their impracticability and criminal folly."

These accusations of Bismarck's could only apply to myself. They referred to my speech on the Commune delivered during the Session of 1871. I attempted to speak, but was "valentined," and was allowed only to make a personal explanation. I rejected as an insult the accusation that I had defended assassins and incendiaries. I had defended those persons because they were not that, but men who had been bitterly wronged. For did not three highly esteemed Governments, those of Switzerland, Belgium, and Great Britain, refuse to allow them to be extradited precisely on the grounds that they were not criminals? I was interrupted by the President and forbidden to continue because my speech went beyond personal explanations and touched upon matters of opinion. But I took my revenge later, at a meeting held in Leipzig, where I thoroughly unburdened my mind.

On the 12th of March, 1876, a debate on the question was arranged in Leipzig between one Bruno Sparig, the chief agitator of the National Liberal party in Leipzig, and myself. The meeting was convened jointly by our two parties, each party receiving a like number of cards, and selecting a chairman to preside while the spokesman of the other side was speaking. My opponent attacked my attitude towards the Commune with the arguments that had been used before. I spoke for about an hour and a half, winding up with the following peroration :—

" The Commune acted as it was bound to act having regard to the state of affairs, and those who do not approve of its action will at least find them explicable and excusable. So much is certain : the Commune has done nothing to be ashamed of, and if it did commit acts of violence the monarchical Governments of Europe when in similar positions have committed acts a hundred times more violent."

In rejoinder, after some quite irrelevant remarks of my opponent's, I said :—

" Sparig has said that as long as Social-Democracy does homage to the phantom of Internationalism his party will have nothing to do with it. Well, we can spare his sympathy. But is Internationalism really a phantom? From the family developed the tribe, from the tribe the State and the nation, and, finally, from a close union of the nations, Internationalism is evolved. This is the course of history. Social-Democracy by adopting the standpoint of universal fraternity, by doing battle against national wars and animosities, and striving to bring the nations together for the work of peace and civilisation—Social-

Democracy stands for the highest ideal of civilisation that it is possible to conceive.

" When our party is insulted to-day because it opposes a narrow national standpoint, sets its face against racial hatred, and upholds the ideal of national fraternisation, it suffers the fate of all pioneers. Gentlemen, here is an example. In a country in which Roman Catholicism predominates you will find the profoundest ignorance concerning Luther.

" All parties all the world over that have stood for progress have suffered the same fate. It was the fate of the Liberals. But to-day, now that the Liberal party is in the ascendant, it regards this world as the best of all possible worlds, and we who speak to a different purpose are treated by them as not quite twenty years ago they themselves were treated by the feudal parties. And naturally so.

" We do not trouble ourselves about these accusations. We know that our time approaches, that circumstances are developing in our favour, that with the disappearance of class antagonism, and the disappearance of the lower middle classes, who are being thrust downward into the ranks of wage-earners, Social-Democracy will grow ever stronger, and will finally lay hands upon the supreme power."

I closed my speech with some remarks as to the attitude of some of the other parties towards our own. " The quarrel between the Conservatives and National Liberals is like a quarrel between husband and wife. As soon as a third party interferes they become reconciled. Some weeks ago a Conservative paper had a leader in which it admonished all opponents of Social-Democracy to unite against the common enemy and to form one great single party of order. Well, we offer our congratulations. You will need to do so. At Chemnitz, too, the Conservatives and National Liberals quarrelled ; each party put up its own candidate. But as soon as it was known that there would be a Socialist candidate as well the quarrel was settled, and the word went round, ' All against Bebel ! ' " With these words of mine the meeting, which had been an immense success, came to an end.

NOTE.—Bebel gives his speech in defence of the Commune, which is very lengthy, *in extenso* in the German text. Stated briefly, his defence amounts to the plea that most of the acts of violence were committed either before the regular Government of the Commune was instituted or after it had been dissolved. Further, if it did commit any atrocities it did so in self-defence, under the stress of necessity and practically under conditions of war, when its existence was threatened by the Versailles army.

The shooting of Generals Lecomte and Clement Thomas was not ordered by the Government of the Commune—which had not then been constituted—but by mutinous troops. Further,

3. More Prosecutions.

In spite of prosecutions the party was in capital fettle, and actively preparing for the next Reichstag elections, which were expected in January, 1877. Our comrades in Berlin had founded a paper of their own, the *Berlin Free Press*, which very soon won the esteem of friend and foe alike.   The first signs of a change in the general policy of the Empire soon evinced themselves.   With the dismissal of von Delbrück, a Free Trade member of the Government, the sudden *volte-face* towards a policy of Protection was inaugurated. Von Camphausen, another Minister, who a few weeks earlier had justified the reduction of wages as a means of overcoming the industrial crisis, and had been praised by the Radical Free Trader Eugen Richter as a man who had the courage to state unpopular truths, soon followed him into the wilderness.

In the meantime there were more prosecutions, especially for libelling the Chancellor.   Bismarck used to have hectograph copies made of actions

the shooting of the hostages, and the burning of the Ministry of Finance, were not ordered by the Government of the Commune. Bebel especially defends Ferre and Raoul Rigault.   On the other hand, he praises the Commune for many measures which it introduced, such as the abolition of night-work in the bakehouses, the separation of Church and State, and the cutting down of official salaries.

for libel, stacks at a time, so that he had one ready the moment any one was denounced to him by the Public Prosecutor. He was continually bringing such actions, right up to the time of his dismissal in 1890. Their number was legion—it ran into thousands—and greatly helped to increase the population of the prisons. These proceedings were certainly no proof of his magnanimity, and were regarded with disapproval even by his warmest admirers.

Tessendorf continued his series of prosecutions. When he dissolved the General German Labour Union he had exclaimed : " Let us destroy the socialistic organisation and the Socialist party will cease to exist ! " Such was his ignorance of the real significance of the movement. His next attack was upon the Socialist-Labour Party. He obtained a decision of the Berlin courts which closed the membership list of the party in Berlin as well as for the whole of Prussia. The party executive admonished the members not to be downhearted. The section of the party thus destroyed was replaced by local organisations—nominally independent—which did more to circulate the party paper and to collect money than the former organisations had ever done.

A party Congress in the proper sense of the word being thus impossible, it was agreed to convene a General Socialist Congress, and in order to render it possible for our Prussian comrades to pay their contributions to the party funds in a manner not amenable to the law a monthly sheet, entitled *The Voter*, not much larger than the palm of the hand, was printed and sold at twopence, with excellent results to the party funds.

When after twenty-six months Most was liberated from Plötzensee prison, near Berlin, he wrote a pamphlet, entitled "The Bastille of Plötzensee," in which he related his experiences, and told how he and other prisoners had managed to hoodwink the prison authorities and make themselves comfortable. It was very imprudent, for the result was an official investigation, and in consequence a much severer treatment of prisoners. The political prisoners were interned in the "Masken-Quartier," so called because prisoners had, during their regulation walks, to wear black masks, in order that no one should recognise them. The pains and penalties became so numerous that finally they caused hardly any sensation ; every editor of a Socialist paper and every agitator knew that it was, so to speak, part and parcel of his calling to go to prison from time to time. At the time I exchanged many letters with Georg von Vollmar, later the leader of the Bavarian Socialist Party. Von Vollmar, who was a retired officer and had been wounded in the Franco-German War, had serious apprehensions that he might lose his pension on account of the many prosecutions in which he became involved, and asked my advice. My counsel, Freytag, who had defended me at the time of my trial in Leipzig, was unable to answer the question definitely, but advised Von Vollmar to be very careful as to what he wrote.

We had, on the other hand, a slight revenge upon one of our persecutors. The highest court of Brunswick condemned General Vogel von Falkenstein—who in 1871 had arrested our executive and sent them in chains to Lötzen—to pay substantial indemnities: to Brucke £105, to others £5 5s., to another 7s. 6d. per diem, and to the workman Kützer 3s. per diem.

4. THE PARTY CONGRESS AT GOTHA IN 1876.

The sixth Congress of the party was held at Gotha on the 19th to 23rd August. The official *Norddeutsche Allgemeine Zeitung* made a good deal of noise, and threatened prosecution, as the Congress was a circumvention of the law. But we did not trouble ourselves, only deciding to use every means of rendering the blows directed against us innocuous.

The Congress was attended by 98 delegates, representing 38,254 members from 291 different localities. The party budget—53,973 marks—(an income of some £2,698 and an expenditure of some £2,721), showing a slight deficit, was balanced by a surplus from the sale of *The Voter*, as mentioned earlier in this chapter. The party then possessed twenty-three newspapers, eight of which were dailies. As a proof of international solidarity it was decided to take suitable means to collect money for those Communards who were in distress. The debates made it obvious that there were still decided differences within the party on personal and party matters. Thus Frohme, a former Lassallean, gave voice to the accusation that several party papers, as well as Liebknecht and myself, had received monetary assistance from Sonnemann, the proprietor of the Radical-Democratic *Frankfurter Zeitung*. I told the Congress that during my imprisonment I had received from Sonnemann, for business purposes, a loan of £90, on which I paid 5 per cent. interest, and which I repaid by instalments. I maintained that the matter was purely personal, the more so as I had been a friend of Sonnemann's since 1866. A motion exonerating me from all blame was accepted. I returned the loan in the course of the same year.

There was another discussion as to our party organ, and finally it was decided by a small minority that the *Volksstaat* of Leipzig should be

the party organ, and should be known as *Vorwärts*.
Liebknecht was to be the editor.

This was the first time the Congress busied itself
with the economic questions of the day. The
industrial crisis, which began in the year 1874,
and became yearly more intense, had brought about
a complete revolution in industrial circles in the
matter of Free Trade or Protection, and finally
converted even the landowners, who had for
decades been the chief defenders of Free Trade.
At first it was principally the iron industry which
protested against the abolition of the duties on
iron, which was to take effect from the 1st of
January, 1877. Other industries, especially the
cotton industry, joined forces with it ; and as,
on account of the competition of American grain,
which was growing more and more considerable,
the prices of grain could not be maintained, the
great landowners of the east of Prussia, who were
losing their export trade through American competition, and were even suffering from a similar
competition in their inland trade, went over to
the Protectionists. These revolutions of opinion
naturally occupied the party, and some members
—Auer and others—had declared for a more or
less complete policy of Protection. The Congress
had to define its attitude, and did so in a rather
lame and unsatisfactory resolution to this effect :

" The Socialists of Germany are not interested in the fight between Free Trade and Protection which has arisen within the ranks of the propertied classes. The question is merely one of expediency, to be decided in each instance upon its merits : the troubles of the working-classes have their root in the general economic conditions as a whole. Yet as the present commercial treaties are un-favourable to German industry they must be amended. The party Press must warn workers not to pull the chestnuts out of the fire for the bourgeoisie, which under the cloak of Protection wishes to capture the State for its own ends."

Another question of the day was the nationalisa-tion of the railways, which had been planned by Bismarck. The Congress declared in favour of nationalisation, but against acquisition by the Empire, because such acquisition would serve only the interests of the aristocratic and militarist State ; the revenue would be wasted on unproductive ex-penditure whereby the Empire would acquire further power—a power hostile to democracy ; and great sums of money belonging to the nation would fall into the hands of the market-riggers of the Bourse.

NOTE.—The railways, in the opinion of the Congress, should become the property of the various Federal States, not of the Empire.

5. The Election Campaign of 1876-7.

For use during the electoral campaign I wrote a small pamphlet as before, which was published in Berlin by the co-operative printers, under the very eyes of Tessendorf, who did not fail to profit by the occasion, as he made us feel later on.

I took a very active part in the campaign, travelling from Leipzig to Cologne and from Cologne to Königsberg, on the eastern frontier, and on to Breslau, everywhere addressing crowded meetings. At Leipzig I addressed a meeting on the question of "the position of women in the present State and with regard to Socialism." Although we had taken the largest hall, many had to be turned away for lack of room. There were many women among the audience. I explained to these that they ought to take the keenest interest in the coming elections, and as so far they had no votes they should take part in the work of agitation, get their husbands and other male relatives to the poll, and make them vote for the Socialists as the only party that stood for the complete social and political equality of the sexes. The meeting was a great success; it was the first at which women were asked to take their part in an electoral campaign.

I was a candidate in my old constituency, Glauchau-Meerane, and in Dresden. I was elected outright in the former constituency, as had been generally expected, and in Dresden got into the second ballot with a Liberal. In this I won by 10,837 votes as against 9,970, and for Dresden I chose to sit. I wrote to a friend at the time: "It greatly tickles me to think that just fourteen years ago to-day I started on my wanderings as a journeyman on the tramp. And now I am Member of Parliament for the royal residence of Dresden. To adapt Napoleon's saying: 'Every artisan on the road has now a mandate for Parliament in his knapsack.' We are getting on—thanks to our friend the enemy."

The elections were highly favourable to us. Altogether twelve Socialists were elected. The votes obtained by our party had increased from 351,070 in 1874 to 493,447 in 1876—that is, an increase of 141,777 votes, or 36 per cent.

In Saxony our party received the greatest aggregate number of votes—124,600 out of 318,740.

The "Tessendorf system" had proved a complete failure. And although the prosecutions directed against the party and its Press became more and more violent, and the courts more draconic in their judgments against us, it availed them nothing. Nor was Bismarck more successful even when, favoured by circumstance, he induced the Reichstag to pass the extremely trenchant measure of coercion which he had wanted all along as a weapon to be used against the party he feared and hated.

The Reichstag of 1877 devoted much of its time to social questions. The Centre,* much alarmed by the steady increase of Social-Democratic votes, started on its proposals of social reform, in the course of which it assumed the likeness of a man who has to dance blindfolded through rows of eggs. Before our successes the attitude of the Centre towards social questions had been rather negative. The measure now introduced by the Centre was intended to improve the condition of small traders and working-men. A party friend had assisted me in working out another measure, as against that proposed by the Centre, which recommended the restriction of the work done in the prisons to work done for the Government; the prohibition of Sunday work in factories; or where that was impossible the observance of one holiday in each week; a normal working-day of nine hours, or eight hours in the case of women and male workers under eighteen; the prohibition of night work, or where that was impracticable the introduction of an eight-hours' shift; a longer period of abstention from work for women before and after childbirth; the introduction, in every factory and

* The Centre party depends upon the votes of the lower middle classes and a section of the workers.

workshop, of a set of regulations, to be agreed upon by employers and employed ; the abolition of " workbooks " for miners ; a character to be given only on demand of the worker ; equal terms of notice for employer and employed ; the prohibition of the truck system ; better protection against accidents ; the introduction of Labour Chambers and Labour Courts ; an Imperial Inspection of Labour under the administration of the Imperial Board of Health ; and, finally, the security and further development of the rights of combination. The debate on the measure introduced by the Centre and our own became a debate on Socialism. I had occasion energetically to reject the accusations levelled against us, and to criticise as it deserved the so-called " Christian " standpoint of the Centre. My speech made a great impression, and the Printers' Trades Union in Leipzig presented me with a beautifully bound copy of it. Of course these debates had no practical results. On the question of the iron duties Bracke made a fine speech, in which he dealt with the problem of Free Trade or Protection ; but the votes of the party were divided, a minority asking for the duties.

Tessendorf had entered an action against me on account of the above-mentioned pamphlet on the elections. But a majority of the Reichstag voted for a motion to stop the action during the

Session. A search at the offices of the *Berlin Free Press* revealed the presence of twelve copies—all that were left.

6. THE CONGRESS AT GOTHA, 1877. ELECTIONS TO SAXON DIET. THE "ZUKUNFT" NEWSPAPER.

As in the year before, the Socialists in the Reichstag convened a general Congress of German Socialists to meet at Gotha, from the 27th to the 30th of May. On account of the laws affecting association and combination it was impossible to call a Party Congress. The report which Auer communicated to the Congress mentioned that the party had put up candidates in 175 out of 397 constituencies. The party papers numbered 41 ; there were also 14 party printing establishments. The revenue amounted to £2,700 and the expenditure to £2,531. Congress adopted the following resolution :—

"In consequence of the most barefaced denial of justice to socialistic organisations as practised with unprecedented impudence by the Prussian authorities, this Congress desists from the creation of party organisations which would come under the Prussian Laws of Association, but it recommends its members to form local organisations suitable to the local conditions."

It has to be noted that the whole of the Liberal

Press, and even the Radical portion of it, did not utter a word of protest against the annoyances, petty persecutions, and violence practised against the Socialist organisations. The authorities regarded this absence of criticism as approval and continued their policy.

Some very disagreeable disputes took place ; one in respect of comrade Hasselmann, who had started, in competition with *Vorwärts,* a paper of his own, the *Red Flag*, which did us great damage and seemed to be working expressly for a split in the party. He was asked by the Congress to cease the publication of his paper.

Another discussion was in respect of a series of articles by Friedrich Engels, attacking Professor Dühring. These appeared in *Vorwärts*. The Professor had vigorously attacked the present condition of things and had declared in favour of communism. He had a great deal of influence with the party in Berlin, and I was of opinion that his writings were to be recommended and exploited in the party interest. His books had been sent me by Bernstein, in 1874, while I was in prison, and I had even published two articles on him and them in *Vorwärts*, entitled " A New Communist." When Dühring, in June, 1877, was censured on account of his doctrines by the University authorities and finally dismissed, his influence with us became all the greater. A resolution was adopted by Congress which forbade *Vorwärts* to publish articles of the nature of Engels' articles attacking Dühring. It is true that the professor finally lost all his influence with the party, such an autocrat did he become; he was so overbearing that his adherents left him one by one.

Von Volmar proposed that a delegate should be sent to the International Socialist Congress at Ghent, in order to give expression to the solidarity of the Socialists of all countries. Although Liebknecht warned the Congress that there was a great danger that the Bakunin-Anarchist movement, which was then at its height in Belgium, would certainly attempt to dominate the Congress, it was resolved to send a delegate. But none went, as in the meantime the party was occupied with different and more important internal affairs.

In 1877 we succeeded for the first time in getting a member of our party elected to the Saxon Diet. Liebknecht was elected for the district of Leipzig. I had been offered the seat, but declined; I could not very well expect my partner to spare me for the sittings of the Saxon Diet as well as for those of the Reichstag. After the election it was found that Liebknecht, not having the necessary qualification of three years' residence in Saxony, could not take his seat; so a second election was held, when

Otto Freytag, the barrister who had been my counsel, was elected.

A weekly paper, the *Zukunft,* was founded in Berlin. It was financed by Karl Höchberg, the son of a Frankfort banker. Höchberg had joined the movement, if I may say so, from motives of sentimental philosophy ; Eduard Bernstein, resigning his position in a Berlin bank, became his secretary. The rather indeterminate attitude of this paper in respect of scientific Socialism as defined by Marx and Engels—it opened its columns to all the various currents of opinion which characterised our movement—excited, from the start, the suspicions of the "two oldsters in London" ; suspicions which deepened when the course of events and the financial difficulties of the party forced us to accept the financial assistance of Höchberg. Marx and Engels, who were too far away to hold a correct view of persons and things, saw in these large sacrifices on the part of Höchberg nothing but a Machiavellian design to entrap the party and divert it from its true aims. They were quite mistaken. Höchberg never made any conditions ; he gave freely, because he had the good of the cause at heart, and never without consulting me or other friends. But in order to allay their suspicions Bernstein and I had late in 1880 to undertake the journey to London which has

since become famous under the name of our
"pilgrimage to Canossa." But I must leave that
to a later chapter.

I myself wrote several articles for the *Zuknuft*,
among them one on "Proportional Representation,"
a subject then little discussed by the party. My
treatment of the question was not approved of by
our old friend Karl Bürkli, then the protagonist
of the system in Switzerland. But I had the satisfaction when I met him, shortly before his death,
in 1901, at Zurich, to hear from his own mouth—
he was then seventy-nine years of age—the confession that I had been right.

7. Ripe for Prison once more.

On the 12th of June, 1877, I appeared before
the notorious Seventh Court of Berlin. Tessendorf
had found in my pamphlet no less than three
separate libels against Bismarck, in addition to
offences against Paragraph 131 of the penal code—
that is, I had published fictitious or misleading
facts knowing them to be such, in order to make
existing public institutions appear contemptible.
Bismarck most willingly gave his consent to the
action. I certainly did not deal tenderly with the
Chancellor in my pamphlet. But when I wrote
it I was still hot with indignation because the
Reichstag had not allowed me to reply to Bis-

marck's most offensive attacks, and had cut short my speech. The offence against Paragraph 131 lay in my manner of attacking militarism. But I felt it as a personal affront that these opinions should be called fictitious and misleading, as Paragraph 131 has it. They were the opinions I had always held and expressed ; what I had written was the honest expression of my standpoint and conviction.

Tessendorf, as Public Prosecutor, took his task very easily. He knew his court, and quite coolly, in a speech of barely five minutes, he asked for a sentence of nine months' imprisonment for the libels against the Chancellor, and of five months for the second offence, which terms might together be reduced to one year.

His nonchalance increased my indignation. I made my own defence, in a speech of one hour and a half in duration. I especially protested against the application of Paragraph 131, because, I stated, it must be known to the court that my attack upon militarism was not fictitious and misleading, but corresponded with my party standpoint and my private convictions, and was supported by quotations from scientific and military authorities.

I think I made a very good speech. But I could not have made any impression on the judges, even without the hailstorm outside, which occupied their attention far more than my fine arguments. The court gave me nine months. I appealed to the higher court. The Public Prosecutor pleaded for confirmation of the sentence of the lower court, especially as I had been condemned before. I again made my own defence, in a speech which lasted an hour, and vigorously protested against the Public Prosecutor's plea that I was a sort of recidivist criminal, and on that account to be severely punished. "A political offender," I said, "should not be put on a level with a common felon. A political offender, even if recidivist, acts from motives of idealism, and merits not severer punishment, but rather approbation, because he acts from conviction." The result was that the indictment in regard to Paragraph 131 was dropped, and I got six months for libel against Bismarck.

I will just add that a few months later the Conservative social reformer Dr. Rudolf Meyer was condemned to one year's imprisonment for libel by the same court, but the Public Prosecutor expressed the pious hope that this would be the last action of Bismarck's. But these actions continued as long as Bismarck was Chancellor—that is, for thirteen years longer.

In order to be near my family and business, I applied to the authorities for permission to pass the last five months of my sentence in the Leipzig Prison.   When I went to the President of the Seventh Court, I was received, to my utter astonishment, with exquisite politeness, and my request was readily granted.

On the 23rd of November I was sent to Plötzensee, the prison near Berlin where most political prisoners were sent, in order to pass the first month of my sentence.   I was allowed to occupy myself with writing, and was granted a light in my cell up to ten o'clock at night.   But Marx's " Capital " and other socialistic writings were confiscated—as though I had not yet been thoroughly corrupted !   The inspector prescribed that I was not to devote the whole of my time to the reading of books, but should at least present some proof of real application.   I therefore wrote a small pamphlet which appeared under the title " France in the Eighteenth Century."

We were not allowed to buy our food from outside, but had to content ourselves with the usual prison fare.   What made this food almost intolerable was the exceedingly restricted bill of fare. The weekly menu for breakfast, dinner, and supper remained exactly the same, without the slightest change.   I lost heavily in weight during the two months I was at Plötzensee.   I cannot understand how the prison doctors can approve of such monotony. Later on the doctor allowed me, at my own request, so-called sick diet. In consequence, I received three times a week a dish of really good meat broth, and a small piece of meat, which was stuck on a wooden skewer because prisoners were not trusted with knives and forks. The piece of meat in the broth was nicknamed "the sparrow," as in shape and size it resembled a plucked sparrow.

I had hoped to be allowed to move to Leipzig just before Christmas, and to pass the holidays with my family. Of the eight Christmas Days my little daughter had so far seen I had passed four in prison. In reply to my application, I was told that all the space in the prison was occupied. I had to wait, and did not reach Leipzig until the 18th of January, 1878.

While at Plötzensee the prison chaplain several times called on me. Most had just then, as I learned from the *Vossische Zeitung,* which I was allowed to read, getting the six numbers all together at the end of each week, started an agitation in Berlin in favour of further secession from the Established (Evangelical) Church. His meetings were crowded, and the excitement was intense. The excitement increased when the Christian Social party, which had lately been founded by Court Chaplain Stöcker, called opposition meetings, or sent speakers to

Most's meetings, where they naturally got the worst of it, amid the general applause of the audience. This agitation made an immense stir among orthodox believers, and our chaplain was greatly excited. Even old Emperor William alluded to the matter in his reply to the President of the Diet, who brought him the congratulations of the Chamber on his birthday, saying, "The religion of the people must be preserved."

8. INTERNAL AFFAIRS.   IN PRISON AT LEIPZIG.

While I was in prison some very significant events transpired. In the place of their party organisation, dissolved by the police, our comrades in Berlin formed a society for the protection of the interests of the working-classes. The Christian Conservative State Socialists founded a weekly paper, the *State Socialist*, with Professors Schäffle, von Scheel, Adolf Wagner, Samter, and others as contributors. These Protestant social reformers were anxious to keep abreast of the Roman Catholic reformers, and as far as possible to save as many of the workers from Social-Democracy as could still be saved.

The approaching revolution in the fiscal policy of the Empire made further strides. The direct contributions of the Federal States to the Budget of the Empire became more and more difficult to raise. Bismarck hated direct taxation. In a speech delivered in 1876 he spoke as follows on the subject of what he considered to be the ideal of taxation :—

" I assure the House that I have a decided prefer- ence for indirect taxation [for the Empire]; I think direct taxation a harsh and clumsy makeshift, with the sole exception of what I venture to call an *Anstandsteuer* [a tax which feelings of decency would compel one to pay], a tax which I shall always maintain : I mean an income tax falling on the rich—that is, on the really rich. I am very anxious to increase the taxes on tobacco, though I certainly do not grudge the smoker his enjoyment of the weed [Bismarck was himself a heavy smoker]. The same principle applies to beer, spirits, sugar, paraffin, and all the other important articles of consumption which are, so to speak, the luxuries of the great mass of the people."

There was some hope that with the help of the Liberals, Bismarck might, by such taxation, pro- vide for the growing needs of the Empire. He had just then a quarrel with the Conservatives, and was not yet reconciled to the Centre. He therefore approached the National Liberals and offered their leader a seat in the Ministry. But the offer fell through, as the National Liberals wanted guarantees against a reactionary policy, which Bismarck could not give. He never forgave them for this refusal.

Berlin was about this time the scene of two events which made a deep impression. August Heinsch, the manager of the Berlin Co-operative Printing Press, died. He was not a great orator, but a most excellent organiser, and enjoyed the utmost confidence of the working-classes of Berlin. His funeral was the occasion of a great Social-Democratic demonstration, such as Berlin had not yet witnessed. The demonstration was attended with the most perfect order and discipline, which greatly impressed our enemies. *Kladderadatsch* * even celebrated the occasion in a poem.

A few weeks later Berlin saw a second funeral, which was even more impressive. Paul Deutler, the responsible editor of the *Berlin Free Press*, had died of consumption, but the accompanying circumstances had been such that a storm of indignation swept through the party in Berlin and through the whole of Germany. He had been condemned for *lèse-majesté* and other offences to twenty-one months' imprisonment, but had appealed. He requested to be released on account of the state of his health. After weeks of delay, and only a short time before his death, he was sent

* The Berlin *Punch*, but strictly political, and a harder hitter.

to the prison ward of the Berlin Hospital. He
died soon after, and his funeral was a fiery protest
against the treatment meted out to him. Again the
crowds astonished and frightened the bourgeoisie.
Thus the *Magdeburger Zeitung* (a National Liberal
paper) said at the time :—

"Who will speak of labour batallions after seeing
this funeral? There were regiments, brigades,
divisions, nay, whole army corps, which paid the
last honours to one who had certainly well deserved
them by his work for the cause."

Since then Berlin has seen many a Social-Democratic funeral, attended by yet vaster crowds, who
shouted their "*Mene, Tekel, Upharsin*" into the
ears of the bourgeoisie.

The Reichstag assembled on the 6th of April,
1878. I was in prison, and my request that I
should be released was not granted. During one
of the debates upon Socialists and their doings—
and such debates were frequent—Bismarck had had
the bad taste to remark, jokingly, that he was quite
willing to make over some district in Prussian
Poland to me as a trial ground for socialistic
experiments. I am sorry I was not in my place to
reply to his jest in a fitting manner.

I used my leisure in prison to write an article
for *Vorwärts* advocating the creation of a general
party library ; this plan was put into execution,

but much later. I completed my book on "Women and Socialism," the first edition of which was issued in the following year. I also wrote a pamphlet on "The Imperial Board of Health," in which I discussed the problem of social hygienics, which the Board had to solve if it was to justify its name.

I had the opportunity of somewhat improving the lot of my fellow-prisoners. I learned, in private conversation with my warder, that the inspector of the prison had grown rich by selling food and drink to prisoners who had money; further, that he economised in soap and handkerchiefs, and made other illicit profits. I sat down and wrote a letter of complaint to the president of the court which had the supervision of the prisons. I wrote the letter as if coming from a prisoner who had just been released. Of course, the letter was to be anonymous. When next my wife visited me I managed to slip a note into her hand, asking her to walk along the street on which the window of my cell opened punctually at half-past nine the next day. I would then throw out a letter, which she was to have copied by an unknown hand and to send to the director of the prison. Everything was done as I had planned. A few days later the warder told me excitedly that the director had paid an unexpected visit to the prison, and had had a violent scene with the inspector. He had read him extracts from the letter of a former prisoner, and the inspector had at once ordered the warders to set things in order. Of course, I did not reveal my secret.

CHAPTER XIX

THE EVE OF THE ANTI-SOCIALIST LAWS

1. THE ATTEMPT ON THE LIFE OF THE EMPEROR AND ITS CONSEQUENCES.

On the 12th of May the news was brought me in my cell—it was news that utterly surprised me—that at three o'clock in the afternoon of the day before a certain Hödel, of Leipzig, a Social-Democrat, had made an attempt upon the life of the old Emperor, but that the Emperor had escaped unharmed. At first the whole affair was a mystery to me. I remembered the name Hödel, *alias* Lehmann. A year earlier he had become known in party circles—I did not personally know him—and as he had no work, perhaps did not want any—he was by trade a tinsmith—he had busied himself with the sale of our local party organ, the *Torch*, and other Socialist literature. But he was exposed as a swindler. He embezzled the money he received, and was dismissed by the management; this was on the 5th of April. The Leipzig party members had decided upon his expulsion from the party, and this expulsion was actually announced on the 9th of May in *Vorwärts*.

After his dismissal he had applied to the *Leipziger Tageblatt* and the National Liberal agent, Sparig, and had sold them a string of false and exaggerated accusations against our party which they attempted to use against us. Then they gave him money to take him to Berlin. In Berlin he exploited both sides; he joined a Social-Democratic society, and at the same time the Christian Social party of Stöcker, which at that time opened its doors to a number of Catilinarian individuals, among them a tailor, Grüneberg, who had been expelled from the party at Munich and Stuttgart on account of fraud. Grüneberg stated that Dr. Nobiling, the man who made the second attempt on the Emperor's life, had also been a member of the Christian Social party. In Berlin, Hödel peddled Social-Democratic as well as Christian Social papers and literature. When arrested photographs of Liebknecht and Most were found upon him, which he used to sell.

As soon as Bismarck received the news of the attempt made by Hödel he telegraphed to Berlin, " Coercion laws against the Socialists." Such was his longing to give the death-blow to the party he hated. However, the public and the Press took the news rather coolly at first; and when some of the papers charged the Social-Democrats with the attempt the semi-official *Hamburger Korrespondent* stated that in the last seventy-eight years many attempts had been made on the lives of notable personages, but by men of many different parties. To saddle Social-Democracy with political murder was unjust.

Hödel, when on his trial, denied the attempt ; he had really intended to commit suicide. When he was arrested he had not a penny in his pocket, and the pistol he used was a quite useless affair, which, as experts witnessed, would not carry more than a few yards. It was found that Hödel was born out of wedlock, and was poorly educated. His head had been filled with Bible and Catechism verses, but he could not write a correct sentence. He had the laugh of an idiot ; he laughed on entering court and on receiving the sentence of death. It was found that he had been a liar and thief from his youth. His whole conduct was that of a degenerate. Yet he was condemned to death, and on account of such a man was German Social-Democracy to be crucified !

2. THE FIRST " EXCEPTIONAL " OR COERCION LAW.

Bismarck's desire for a coercion law affecting Socialists was rapidly incorporated in a Bill. It reached the Reichstag on the 20th of May and was to be debated on the 23rd.

The National Liberals were very uneasy. The Prussian Ministry had, by the elimination of all Liberal members, been transformed into a re-actionary body. The Bill, consisting of six clauses, embodied the following restrictions on Socialism : Literature and associations of Social-Democratic tendencies could be prohibited by the Federal Council,* but the prohibition had to be communi-cated to the Reichstag as soon as it assembled, and had to be cancelled on demand of that body. The police were empowered provisionally to prohibit the sale of literature in the streets, squares, and other public places. The prohibition was to be cancelled if within four weeks it was not formally proclaimed by the Bundesrat. The prohibition and dissolution of meetings lay wholly in the hands of the police without appeal. Contraventions of these prohibitions were to be punished with im-prisonment for terms of not over five years' duration. Printed matter could be seized without a judicial decision. The presidents of prohibited associations and the promoters and chairmen of meetings which had been proclaimed and the owners of premises hired for such meetings were to be punished with not less than three months' imprisonment. The law was to be in force for three years.

* The Federal Council (*Bundesrat*) represents the Govern-ments of the individual States of Germany ; its members (58) are appointed by these Governments.

Thinking that the party in the Reichstag would vigorously attack the measure, I wrote to them from prison : "The Member who speaks on our side ought to consider that his speech will be distributed in hundreds of thousands of copies, and will probably be used as an election pamphlet when the Reichstag is dissolved, if the Bill should be rejected. It is very important that everything that can be said against Hödler should be carefully considered."

But the party decided, after long deliberation, not to take part in the debate, but only to make a formal declaration. This was pronounced by Liebknecht, and was to this effect : "The attempt to make use of the deed of a madman, even before the judicial investigation is closed, as a pretext for the execution of a reactionary coup planned long before, and to saddle with the 'moral authorship' of a yet unproved murderous attempt upon the German Emperor a party which condemns murder of every kind and regards economic and political development as quite independent of the will of individual persons—this attempt carries with it its own condemnation in the eyes of all unprejudiced people ; so much so that we, the representatives of the Social-Democratic electors of Germany, are urged by necessity to make the following declaration :—

" We regard it as beneath our dignity to take part in the debates on this exceptional law now before the Reichstag, and shall not allow our resolution to be shaken by any provocations from whatever side they may come. But we shall take part in the actual voting, because we think it our duty to put our votes in the balance, in order to do all that is possible on our part to prevent an unprecedented attack upon the liberties of the people.

" Whatever the decision of the Reichstag, the Social-Democracy of Germany, inured to conflict and persecution, views the coming persecution and conflict with the quiet confidence that the consciousness of a just and unconquerable cause confers."

After Liebknecht, Bennigsen, the leader of the National Liberals, spoke. He made a good speech— I think the best he ever made. He referred to the then unstable position of the Ministry. In Prussia a Cabinet crisis seemed to have become a permanent institution. Before giving dictatorial power to any one it was important to consider to whom it would be given. His party would not consent to " exceptional laws " such as the present one ; history shows to what they lead, and that they are never productive of good. But he offered the assistance of his party in the assurance of civic liberty and firm authority, but only on the ground of a common law for all. At the division the first clause was rejected by 243 votes against 60. The Centre voted in its favour, but of the National Liberals only three professors did so: Beseler, von Gneist, and von Treitschke. The Government went no further, but dropped the measure. But the Minister of the Interior urged the police to use their power with the utmost rigour—an injunction they were only too ready to obey.

3. Nobiling's Attempt on the Life of the Emperor and its Results. Elections of 1878.

By the end of May I was released from prison. On the 2nd of June, a Sunday, I returned home from a walk with my family at about seven in the evening, when a sister of Freytag's the barrister hurried into the room and asked excitedly if we had heard the news. We lived in the suburbs, to which news filtered but slowly. Confessing our ignorance, Miss Freytag continued: "Do you know Dr. Nobiling? He has this afternoon shot the Emperor and dangerously wounded him." I was speechless, as though struck by lightning, but finally answered that I had never heard his name, and thought it out of the question that he was a member of our party. Miss Freytag went away quite comforted.

Next morning I went to the offices of *Vorwärts*.

I found a public telegram which contained nothing to the effect that Nobiling belonged to the party. We all breathed more freely, and were thankful that the party could not be held responsible. None of us knew him ; no one had heard his name before. I left the office, but returned a few minutes later. A second telegram had been published stating that Nobiling had confessed that he was a Social-Democrat and that he had accomplices. We were all speechless.

It was discovered later on that these statements on the part of the Wolff Telegraph Bureau—the German semi-official news agency—and other messages relating to the same affair were grave perversions of the truth. But they did their work only too well. Public opinion, already excited by the news of the 1st of June relating to the sinking of the *Grosser Kurfürst*, one of the largest vessels of the German Navy of those days, which had sunk in broad daylight, after collision, with her crew of five hundred, in sight of the English coast, rose to white heat in consequence of this murderous attempt.

Bismarck rejoiced ; he had the means of dissolving the Reichstag in his pocket, and hoped, after the elections, to have a majority at his disposal for the passing of his exceptional measures and for his policy of Protection.

Nobiling had shot at the Emperor from a window overlooking the street known as "Unter den Linden." Afterwards he had attempted suicide, but failed ; he was cut down by an officer who forced the door of his room. He was unconscious for a time and quite unfit to be questioned. But it was established that he had studied agricultural science at Leipzig, and had shown himself, in the debates in the class of Dr. Birnbaum, one of our most redoubtable opponents. It was the same in Dresden, where he attended the class of Professor Böhmert, who was also our avowed enemy. In Dresden he attacked us in public meetings, and thus became known to members of our party, such as Vollmar. Our members said of him, in answer to questions put in court, that they regarded him as an utterly insignificant blockhead. With the party he had even less to do than Hödel. Some people thought he had been incited to his attempt by the way in which the Press dealt with the personality of Hödel. The opinion that Nobiling, too, was a degenerate was widely held ; even the judge had remarked to an editor : "The picture the papers drew of Nobiling is quite untrue ; he is anything but intelligent ; he is even more stupid than Hödel." When Nobiling died in prison, on the 10th of September, not the smallest proof had been adduced that he had ever had the least connection with our party, or that it had either directly or indirectly influenced his action.

Yet for those who wished to excite the public against us, and who were determined at all costs to exploit these two attempts in the interest of the coercion laws, all these established facts were non-existent. Bismarck used his powerful influence with the Press in order to lash the public into a fanatical hatred of the Social-Democratic party. Others who had an interest in the defeat of the party joined in, especially a majority of the employers. Henceforth our opponents spoke of us exclusively as the party of assassins, or the " Ruin all " party—a party that wished to rob the masses of their faith in God, the Monarchy, the family, marriage, and property. To fight the party and if possible destroy it seemed to them the height of glory. Thousands and thousands of workers who were known to be Social-Democrats were summarily dismissed. The newspapers published in their advertisement columns declarations signed by working-men who engaged themselves for the future not to join any socialistic organisation, not to buy or read Social-Democratic papers, not to pay contributions for Social-Democratic purposes. This terrorism on the part of the employers became so violent that our papers asked members to sign anything they were asked to sign, but afterwards to do as they liked, because, in face of such terrorism, they were not bound to keep such pledges. This terrorism even went farther ; patriotic house-owners gave notice to their Social-Democratic tenants, and restaurant-keepers who for years had been only too glad to have Social-Democrats for their customers asked them to keep off their premises. The editors of our paper in Leipzig, having sent the paper to press, used to resort to a certain restaurant for a glass of beer. Now the owner informed them that he did not want them under his roof. The same thing happened in Berlin and elsewhere.

But these explosions of fanatical boorishness and political insanity were not enough to satisfy the patriots in their frenzy of persecution. A deluge of denunciations of *lèse-majesté*, genuine and fictitious, fell on our devoted heads. In many cases it was proved that the informers were inspired by the spiteful desire of avenging private wrongs. The judges also gave way to this paroxysm of persecution. They almost always passed the maximum sentences prescribed by the law, up to five years' imprisonment.

Early in July the Radical *Vossische Zeitung*, which had printed a list of the sentences passed outside Berlin, stated that they amounted altogether to five hundred or six hundred years of prison.

Altogether, in two months, 521 persons were condemned to 812 years of prison. A small proportion of these were genuine members of the Social-Democratic party. The police, as always in such cases, behaved as if they had lost their wits, making searches and arrests on the vaguest suspicions. The majority of those arrested had almost immediately to be released.

The Town Council of Gotha prohibited the Socialist Congress which was to have met there in June. We were repeatedly told that those in authority had remarked : " The Socialists ought to have their hands tied and be squeezed against the wall until they rebel and can be shot down." The *Berlin Free Press* therefore wrote : " Be careful, comrades ; beware ; they want to shoot you down ! " Yet the number of subscribers to almost all the Socialist papers increased—those of the *Berlin Free Press*, for example, from ten thousand to fourteen thousand in six months.

To me personally and as a business man this universal hatred had very disagreeable results. Shortly after my release I had urgent occasion to travel for my firm in the north-west of Germany and the Lower Rhine districts. It was fortunate that I had never been there before and was not personally known. I went to the hotels under a fictitious name, as if I had used my own no hotel-

keeper would have taken me in. Day by day I
had to listen to the most virulent abuse of our
party and myself. I fared as might be expected
at the hands of the firms when I offered my wares.
A merchant of Halle, pleased with my samples, gave
me a considerable order, but when I gave him
our business card he cancelled it. Others simply
declined to deal with us. When I returned home
after six weeks of travelling I had not earned
enough to cover my expenses, although I kept them
as low as possible and carried my sample trunk,
which weighed about twenty pounds, in order to
save the expense of a porter.

As soon as I was home I was immersed in the
election campaign. Bismarck, who was used to strike
the iron while it was hot, had prevailed upon the
Federal Council to dissolve the Reichstag, although
after the second attempt upon the Emperor even
the Reichstag as it was would have voted a
coercion law by a large majority. But Bismarck
had other aims ; he wanted to break the power
of the National Liberal party and to push his
policy of Protection. In an election address inspired by him he almost proudly broke away from
the economic system which had so far prevailed.
The address stated that the predominance in the
Reichstag of lawyers, officials, and professors—that
is, of persons not directly productive—had given

its debates a theoretical flavour. Party hatred, the lust for power of the various factions, and the ambition of the leaders had made the Reichstag the stage for oratorical performances. The majority of the deputies followed no really productive occupation, neither trade nor industry nor agriculture nor commerce. The representation of the vast national interests was entrusted entirely to the hands of men who were not producers, but lived by salaries, property, stipends, or investments.

The election campaign was more violent than ever before. All the bourgeois parties joined forces against us. "No Social-Democrat in the Reichstag," was the watchword, even in the Radical Press.

I stood for Dresden and Leipzig. In Dresden there was a three-cornered contest between a Liberal, a Conservative, and myself. In the first ballot I received 9,855 votes, the Conservative 7,266, and the Liberal 5,410. In the second ballot between myself and the Conservative—which had been cunningly fixed on the day of the seventieth birthday of my opponent—I was returned at the head of the poll with 11,616 votes against 1,072. In Leipzig I received 5,822 votes, 600 more than at the preceding election. Altogether our party elected nine candidates, but only two at the first ballot.

Thus the Social-Democratic party had not been extirpated from the Reichstag. Even in respect of the number of votes received we fared better than could have been expected after the formidable agitation against us and the terrorism exerted in some constituencies by our opponents. We secured at the first ballot 437,158 votes, which, compared with the 493,447 votes of 1877, showed a loss of only 56,387 votes and three seats.

The result of the election was favourable to Bismarck's policy of Protection. The National Liberals were reduced from 137 Members to 106, the Radicals from 39 to 26. Their loss was the gain of the Conservatives, and to some extent of the Centre.

Bismarck had now two majorities at his disposal —a National Liberal-Conservative majority for his Coercion Bill and a Conservative-Centre majority, supported also by the right wing of the National Liberals, for his Protectionist policy. The new era of the denial of political rights to the class-conscious workers and the burdening of the masses by means of Customs duties could now commence. The new Reichstag was to meet on the 9th of September in order to pass the anti-Socialist laws.

The play was ready to begin. It was intended to be a tragedy, in the course of which the Social-Democratic party was to be sacrificed upon the altar of the monarchical and capitalistic interests. But, as before, it did not "come off"; we turned the tragedy into a comedy, and the Hercules who came forth to strike us down with his bludgeon was himself laid low after an inglorious ten years' war against the hated enemy, and cumbered the field of battle with his corpse.

Whereas in the old days of the Empire the battle cry of the advancing armies was "To me, Guelph! To me, Ghibelline!" it was now "To me, Bismarck! To me, Social-Democrats!"

INDEX

The header contains "342 INDEX"